C000148776

CHAM
TIMES

Yorkshire CCC 1959 - 1968

by Fred Trueman
& Don Mosey

Sponsored by

Foreword

By Viscount Mountgarret
President, Yorkshire CCC 1984-89

I feel very privileged to have been asked to write this foreword to the reminiscences and tales of Yorkshire's golden years in the 1960s. It gives the older generation who watched, or who had anything to do with Yorkshire cricket in those years, the chance to walk down a delightful memory lane. Importantly it has given the younger generation and players of today the chance to gain an insight to the feelings of the great players who took part in these moments of triumph.

It is so easy to harp back and muse that the earlier years of anything, including cricket, were so much better than today, and nurture the feeling "if only things were like that now." There is a danger of falling into the trap of Gilbert's "idiot who praises every century but this and every country but his own."

Times have changed enormously since then which has had a great effect on the game both at county and international level. I feel that the changes that have evolved, or been deliberately made, are not necessarily always to the good. There is a danger of players becoming stale by being required to play so much cricket in the season that there is little time to rest and relax. I am sure that there are some who would hanker after the days when each county played each other twice, at home and away, and have the opportunity over the weekend to relax on a Sunday, following whatever other recreation they so wished. This is the more so at Festival times.

However, with the increasing demands from all quarters, finance has become predominant in people's thoughts, be they administrators or players, each for his own different reasons. That inevitably has its effect.

Having said that, we are at least all in the same boat, and we do now compete with other counties under the same terms and conditions, unlike yesteryear. The stark truth is, however, that Yorkshire teams after 1969 began to decline and until 1981 onwards they never achieved getting into single figures in terms of their County Championship position, except once in 1987, when they won the Benson & Hedges Cup as well. It might also be worth remembering that Yorkshire's position in the championship table was such that from 1873 to 1968 they never dropped to double figures, except on two occasions in 1953 and 1958.

There are, maybe, lessons to be learnt from these unfortunate facts. Being on a par with all other counties, surely somehow some of Yorkshire's former glories might be regained? Indeed, it is said of Lord Hawke that he, in 1883, occupied the position in the British Empire second only to that of Queen Victoria, namely, captain of Yorkshire. Reading this book recording the memories of those who were players in 1959-68, will, I am sure, instil in the players of today and tomorrow an even greater desire to win and achieve the highest honours again that the game can bestow.

Stainley House,
       Harrogate (May, 1994)

Introduction

In the ten seasons between 1959 and 1968, Yorkshire won the county cricket championship on seven occasions. In 1961 they were runners-up, 'pipped' by Hampshire in a season in which the weather played such a part that Yorkshire could only draw ten of their matches.

Even so, they got more bonus points than any other county despite losing the services of Trueman during four Tests, Illingworth (two) and Close (one). In 1964 they finished fifth, in 1965 they were fourth (and won the Gillette Cup).

They were indeed ten glorious years and they were fashioned by a team of Yorkshire-born players with a rather special attitude to the game and their place within it. They argued furiously amongst themselves; occasionally there were major upheavals. Indeed, other counties became used to rows in the dressing-room next door and Yorkshire were widely regarded as unique – not simply because of the insistence on home-bred players only, but because of the apparent disharmony in the ranks on so many occasions.

The Committee of that era did not exactly help. There was an autocratic attitude to the players who seemed to be regarded as some kind of mediaeval mercenaries who were simply being paid to do a specific job and were expected to do it better than anyone else. There was an extraordinary 'Them and Us' gulf between players and committee and, it has to be said, the players were treated for the most part as people without sensitivity, without feelings, without problems. They had no contracts and they did not know, in effect, whether they would have a job from one year to the next. It was not the healthiest atmosphere in which to make such decisions as whether to get married, or buy a house, or start a family. There was no real feeling of security.

The players somehow comforted themselves that once they had been awarded a county cap they stood a reasonable chance of being re-engaged for the following season. It was the only employment straw at which they could clutch. Many of them had no car and to travel up and down the country every Tuesday and Friday night they had to double up with the players who had transport. They did not, by any means, always stay in hotels with four-and five-star conditions of luxury.

Before the 1962 season began there were 13 players with caps and the club chairman, Brian Sellers, gave them this comforting assurance before they set out on the new campaign: "You can be sure there won't be 13 caps *next* season." So for the next four months the players skirmished and battled in the knowledge that one or two of them were going to be sacked by the following September. All except, perhaps, four of the team spent the summer looking anxiously over their shoulders and comparing their figures and achievements with those of their colleagues.

Were these the circumstances and conditions to produce a great team – surely not? And yet the truth is that Yorkshire in the 1960s were indeed a great *team*. This was not a side of necessarily great *players*. Indeed, there was general agreement that they had three, arguably four, truly great players in their own right. But the team, as a team, had become undeniably great as a playing unit. And everyone else in the game recognised this. The visit of Yorkshire was the occasion of the biggest "gate" for every other county. When benefits were awarded in 16 other shires, it was usually the Yorkshire match which was chosen by the beneficiary. All other sides raised their game; no one gave Yorkshire an inch of room to manoeuvre a possible victory. Bowlers saved their best performances for the visit of, or to, Yorkshire; batsmen stored up the runs for when the Tykes came into view.

And out of all this, in spite of so many problems and vicissitudes, Yorkshire fashioned their game within the ranks of 12 or 13 Yorkshiremen. Rows there were; arguments raged long before and even longer after every day's play. But once a Yorkshire side walked out of the pavilion, through the gates and onto the turf, the rows subsided and the arguments ceased. There was now but one objective: to beat the opposition. They were Yorkshiremen; it was expected of them.

These were wonderful, memorable cricketing days. It was my privilege – and I do not choose the word idly or casually – to observe these days at close quarters. I heard the arguments, observed the rows... and admired the supreme professionalism which brought the success of those glory years. Because everyone was devoted to the same cause: to win for Yorkshire.

It was my delight to see wins created out of the most unlikely set of circumstances; to see chinks prised open in the armour and chances emerging where none had seemed likely. Most of all I enjoyed those third afternoons when the opposition had to be winkled out in conditions which seemed all against wicket-taking. It was then that Yorkshire cricket appeared at its most tigerish. If Trueman the block-buster couldn't do it, Illingworth, with all the wiles and cunning of his experience, might be the one. Perhaps Wilson, in that century-old tradition of the Yorkshire slow left-armer, could spring a surprise, or Ken Taylor could dispose of an obdurate batsman when others had failed. It might be Ryan, or Platt or Cowan or Nicholson, who closed up one end and perhaps nipped in where the opposition did not expect a break-through. Or it might be one of the others who appeared fleetingly within the ranks from time to time ... Gillhouley, Bainbridge, Waring ... later Cope and Old towards the end of the decade.

It was marvellous cricket and compulsive watching.

Yorkshire in the 1950s had had many magnificent players – some might argue it was the greatest side, man for man, the county had ever had. But there had been no championship. At the 1956 annual meeting the president, Tom Taylor – with a brutal frankness not often heard from presidents – had named remarkably big names: "Willie Watson, Frank Lowson, Vic Wilson and Doug Padgett ... each scored his 1,000 runs, but performances on many occasions were not convincing; batting was often slow and laboured. Brian Close and Ray Illingworth failed to produce the runs expected."

There was more of the same from one member, Mr. H. Whiteley, who claimed: "It is two years since we brought up the matter of players who don't try, and said they should be dropped. But they are still here. It isn't good enough."

Didn't try? Could these be Yorkshire players about whom Mr. Whiteley was uttering such heresy?

The turning-point came in 1958 with the appointment of Ronnie Burnet as county captain. This was one of the most daring and controversial moves in the history of the club. A few other counties had dispensed with the tradition of an amateur captain but in those days Yorkshire did not idly dispense with traditions.

Ronnie Burnet was 39 years old, a seasoned Bradford League player but one who had never appeared in a first-class match of any kind. He was now asked to weld together a winning team from a group of big names, big personalities, big reputations, all with a sharp awareness of their importance, together with a handful of youngsters, relatively inexperienced, three of whom were newly capped and five uncapped.

It is impossible to exaggerate the problems which confronted Burnet – they were immense – and it is a great pity he has not been persuaded to set out his own version of those two years, 1958 and 1959. Today, 25 years and more later, there are still differing attitudes and opinions on the brief but significant Burnet reign. In historical terms, the "release" by Yorkshire of Johnny Wardle, then the best slow left-arm bowler in the world, has over-shadowed everything else about the period and Burnet's version has never been given publicly, in detail. It would make a fascinating document.

What *is* undeniable, however, is that Yorkshire, after finishing in 11th position in 1958, won the championship the following year – and won it in the most exhilarating and heroic fashion in the final game of the season. The heroes' welcome from far-off Hove was completed at Scarborough the following day. It was a win achieved by scoring 218 in 28.3 overs (or 98 minutes in the parlance of the day) by a team which by now believed whole-heartedly in itself, its leadership and its traditions. To Ronnie Burnet must go a major share of the credit for moulding a team which could do that.

The Dark Ages were over; the Glory Days had begun... and were to continue for the next ten years. Vic Wilson took over the side in 1960 and led Yorkshire to two wins and a second place in this three years as captain. He was followed by Brian Close under whose leadership Yorkshire won the title in 1963 and 1966-67-68 as well as the Gillette Cup in 1965 (and 1969).

These were teams composed entirely of Yorkshire-born players and the county was still "exporting" cricketers of ability to play with other counties. Between 1959 and 1968 they met, playing for other counties, these men: Charlie Lee, Arnold Hamer, David Smith, Peter Chadwick, Billy Oates (with Derbyshire); Bill Greensmith and Gordon Barker (Essex); Barry Wood and Peter Lever (Lancashire); Willie Watson, Jack Van Gelovan, Bernie Cromack, Dickie Bird, Jack Birkenshaw, Peter Broughton and Ray Illingworth (Leics); Don Bennett (Middlesex); Desmond Barrick (Northants); Barrie Whittingham, Mike Smedley, Bill Rhodes, Barry Stead and Brian Bolus (Notts); Graham Atkinson, Lewis Pickles, Tony Clarkson (Somerset); Terry Gunn (Sussex); Norman Horner (Warwicks); Roy Booth (Worcs).

Almost all these players had appeared in Yorkshire's first or second teams before moving on. Some achieved Test status "at home"; others became England players after relocating. There were more before them; more have departed since that time. The most fruitful "nursery" in English cricket has always been Yorkshire and it is impossible to believe that the supply of players has dried up.

The sheer weight of "production" in the 1960s meant there was always serious competition for places. Always, it seemed, there were two groups of three batsmen competing for two places; three or four bowlers for two places. Men played with pain-killing injections to fight off injuries and avoid risking a youngster coming in and perhaps turning in an outstanding performance. And yet – perhaps a trifle paradoxically – there seemed always to be a willingness to help the inexperienced player. Bryan Stott, for instance, remembers the tremendous help given to him by Willie Watson, even though Watson must have sensed the threat from the promise of the younger left-hander. Ask any (now) old player and he will tell you a similar story. It was never written down anywhere; it was never openly stated. But is was all part of doing one's bit for the greater glory of Yorkshire cricket.

In that 1959-68 period a team of home-spun Yorkshiremen beat the whole might of the touring West Indians (Middlesbrough, 1963) and it was a strong enough team to have Joe Solomon batting at No.7 in the order after Frankie Worrell, Joey Carew, Rohan Kanhai, Seymour Nurse, Gary Sobers and Basil Butcher. Five years later, Fred Trueman, leading Yorkshire with enormous pride and great passion, saw victory over Bill Lawry's Australians as the highlight of his Yorkshire career.

Pride! Ah, now there is the essential ingredient when one looks back at the Yorkshire team of the 1960s. It was a special kind of pride which went back to earliest schooldays; it was every sport-minded youngster's ambition to play for Yorkshire. The street-games, the school playground, park-and-recreation ground fixtures, were played in the names of Sutcliffe and Hutton, Bowes and Verity. First came hopes of being called to the Yorkshire nets, of batting and bowling with and against the mighty. Then, perhaps, encouraged strenuously by one's school, might come selection for the Yorkshire Federation XI. Then the Colts... Ah! Where might the path lead from there? There was pride in the player's school, in his club and league; in his family and his town and the valleys.

It's a pretty safe bet that none of the youngsters of that era had money foremost in his mind when he yearned to play cricket for Yorkshire. It never occurred to anyone that within 30 years the humblest, most junior Colt, called up for the first time, might walk boldly into Headingley and ask, "Where is my free, sponsored car?" No, it was a different age with a different sense of history, of values, a different philosophy. It bred a brand of camaraderie which was uniquely wonderful. Arguments would rage, bitterness be expressed, resentment aired; and then the arguers would walk out side by side and play together as if their lives depended on it. Those men of the 1960s would have died for each other on the cricket field. Their attitude to the game was something which other counties could only envy – and marvel at.

Perhaps the attitude of the young man called up for the first time is best summed up by Keith Gillhouley when he was asked if he would like to contribute a memory to this book. He wrote: "A special match? It has to be my first one. That, and the games that followed in 1961, were like a fairy-tale come true. The sense of achievement in actually playing for Yorkshire was heightened by my up-bringing and a very descriptive father. He told me, from my very earliest days, of Hirst and Rhodes, of the captaincy of Brian Sellers, of the deadliness of Verity on a helpful pitch and his accuracy on one that wasn't; of Leyland's famous remark about fast bowling; of Hutton's great innings at The Oval; all of that and much, much more. It made me feel I would never be good enough to play. But he encouraged me..."

There is more of what it meant to Gillhouley to play for Yorkshire in the following pages and it really says it all. It must not, however, be thought that the ten years we are recalling were all grim intensity. The cricket was indeed intense. The modern triumvirate of cricketing wisdom provided by Close, Illingworth and Binks gave expert support to the captain and merited (and achieved) complete respect, even amid a certain amount of banter. There was laughter and there was a sense of fun, even on the days of starkest acrimony. And on the darkest day, when things had gone badly, an evening of song led by Sharpe and Wilson was a splendid antidote.

Oh yes. There was a lot of fun and laughter, as will be seen in later chapters. Laughter was never very far away. But first came the desire, and the need, to win. In many ways it gave county championship matches the atmosphere of Tests and because of the smaller scale of a three-day match the tension was intensified. Only very rarely could spectators claim they didn't get their moneysworth.

Yes – they were Glory Days all right; I rejoice, and am respectfully grateful, that I was able to see so many of them at close quarters. One last thought. Sir William Worsley, President of Yorkshire CCC from 1961 to 1973, was unable to attend the 1968 annual meeting but he sent this message: "Since a number of counties have engaged (overseas) players of Test Match status it will be interesting to see what effect this will have on county cricket. I am sure we are proud of the fact that all our cricketers are Yorkshire-born and I hope we shall never go outside our boundaries to recruit our players. As long as we have the whole-hearted support of the Yorkshire leagues and clubs, the need should never arise."

D.M.

1

Bob
Platt

Derbyshire v Yorkshire
Chesterfield 1959
4th, 6th, 7th July

ROBERT KENWORTHY PLATT, *born 26.12.1932, Holmfirth. Right-hand batsman, right-arm medium-fast bowler. Played in 96 matches for Yorkshire between 1955 and 1963, scoring 424 runs and taking 301 wickets with his in-swing bowling. Took a Minor Counties hat-trick against Notts II and another in Bradford League cricket (Bradford v Idle) with the first three balls of an innings. He had a successful spell as Yorkshire II captain after retiring from the first-class game and later joined the Yorkshire Committee. A director of the family electrical engineering and equipment business in Holmfirth.*

It has to be said: more unkind, distorted and downright inaccurate statements have been made about my batting than about almost anything else in cricket.

I have never actually claimed to be a *great* batsman; what I have said and with, I insist, all due modesty, is that I was seriously under-rated in this area of my cricket. It is no exaggeration to say that I had all the strokes; I could read the spinners accurately (and there were, remember, two or more in every side in the 1950s and 1960s); position myself well; place the ball nicely clear of the field. And it was common courtesy, following a time-honoured tradition, that I didn't expect to find the ball flying at my throat when quick bowlers returned to claim their just reward of a couple of tail-end wickets.

Yet in 1959, with four years first-class experience behind me following my apprenticeship in the Huddersfield League, National Service and the RAF side and Yorkshire II, I was subject to indignities like this piece in the *Daily Mirror*: "Seam bowler Bob Platt's place in the Yorkshire batting order is not settled – except that he shuttles between Nos.10 and 11." And it has to be said that my claims were taken no more seriously in the Yorkshire dressing-room. Indeed, they were dismissed scathingly by people who had really no right to do so.

It was, therefore, necessary for me to exercise patience. My day would come. I was as certain of that as any comedian yearning to play Hamlet. And it came on Monday, 6th July, 1959, at Queens Park, Chesterfield – an appropriately sylvan setting with its lines of trees, its banks of flowers, its lake and its marquees. There was not, I fear, the sort of cheering crowd I would ideally have liked for such an occasion. Monday afternoon in North Derbyshire is not compulsive cricket-watching time, even in high summer. What mattered was that my fellow Yorkies were out in force on the pavilion balcony for the situation was serious.

On the previous Saturday, Derbyshire had declared at 351 for eight – a bit of an impertinence in itself. Derbyshire declaring against Yorkshire! What made it just a bit worse was that two exiles, Charlie

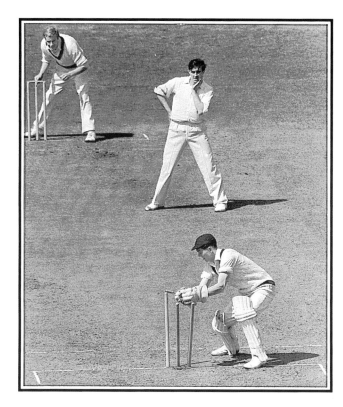

Fred Trueman looks on as Jimmy Binks attempts a run out. (Photo by Colorsport)

Lee and Arnold Hamer, had made 122 of those runs for the first wicket. And now Yorkshire, at 197 for eight, were in danger of the ultimate humiliation – following on.

I felt no fear as I walked out to the middle ... perhaps just a tremor of disquiet that Les Jackson was operating with a second new ball which was still quite shiny – and everyone in the game respected Jacko. But this was my big chance – the opportunity to show those scoffers who had been so free with their advice in the past that this was one comedian who could play Hamlet with style.

The crowd were not encouraging; "soccer-style loudmouths," the *Daily Express* called them. They had actually slow-handclapped Ronnie Burnet a little earlier for playing three balls from Edwin ("Tat") Smith defensively. But now the captain had gone and so had Jimmy Binks. Jack Birkenshaw remained and the only remaining batsman was Chris Wood, a Bradford lad playing for Yorkshire for only the third time. Clearly it was up to me. My time had come.

I executed a flowing off-drive and was rewarded with a stentorian roar from Duggie Padgett on the balcony: "Get your head down!" And *he* scored only four ...

It is unnecessary to labour the point. With a bit of help from Birkenshaw I avoided the follow-on, took afternoon tea in a mood of calm confidence and after the interval, according to the *Daily Express*, "was off in a flurry of fours." This was my dream coming true. The strokes I had so vainly struggled for years to convince my colleagues that I possessed were now unveiled in all their glory. And glorious they were. Donald Carr, the Derbyshire captain, was forced to put himself on. Birkenshaw, in the meantime, had gone but young Chris Wood was doing a noble job as my assistant. I wanted it to go on forever.

Carr went round the wicket and then dropped one short. I stepped back, feet perfectly positioned, saw the ball pitch and turn. Then, "Oh God," I thought, "It's the wrong 'un." It was a situation which called for lightning thought; the bat had been swung in its perfect, curving arc. No time to check; I had to go through with the shot. My timing was superb. With exquisite care, I placed the stroke in front of square-leg and just out of his reach but, quite honestly, I had under-estimated the perfection of my timing. The ball scattered the drinkers and slow-handclappers amongst the marquees. A six. It was, in fact, the only six I hit in my first-class career. But that, of course, was entirely due to the way I kept my strokes on the ground.

Sadly, it could not go on as long as I would have liked. Young Chris – and I cannot speak too highly of his support in a last-wicket partnership of 41 (his share was ten) – succumbed to the wiles of Carr and Yorkshire were all out for 275. Even so, and despite a deficit of 76 on the first innings, Yorkshire won the game by six wickets when Carr was cheeky enough to declare a second time.

The congratulations due to me were delivered with sheepish embarrassment. Perhaps the most enjoyable moment came when Don Carr decreed that because Bryan Stott had not fielded because of injury, he could only bat in the second innings *after all the established batsmen*. It was with some satisfaction that I earnestly informed him: "That means after *me*, Stottie."

But I leave the last word to E.W. Swanton – can one ask for a higher authority? Impressed, perhaps, by my 5-31 against Surrey at The Oval a month earlier, he had made one of his rare journeys northwards and delivered in the *Daily Telegraph*, this verdict from Chesterfield: "Anyone arriving late on the ground and watching him (me) stroke the ball handsomely through the covers could have taken him for a reputable No.5 bat. He finished with 57 not out, his previous best having been 17, and I cannot begin to explain why it was not many more."

I can, Jim. It's not easy to make runs at Nos.10 and 11.

At the end of the season I scanned the Yorkshire averages. In last place came the name of R.K. Platt: 29 innings, 13 not outs, highest score 57*, total runs 130, average 8.12.

As someone once said (I think it was Mark Twain): "There are three kinds of lies: lies, damned lies and statistics." He was wrong. There are four kinds – add on "the Yorkshire averages."

DERBYSHIRE

First Innings		Second Innings	
A. Hamer b Platt	67	c and b Birkenshaw	33
C. Lee c Wood b Illingworth	64	c Illingworth b Birkenshaw	44
J. Kelly c Padgett b Illingworth	19	c Bird b Illingworth	10
D.C. Morgan c Birkenshaw b Platt	25	c Binks b Birkenshaw	28
D.B. Carr run out	65	not out	74
H.L. Johnson b Birkenshaw	32	not out	17
G.O. Dawkes c and b Illingworth	2	) did not bat	
I. Buxton lbw b Illingworth	1	)	
G.W. Richardson not out	44	b Platt	13
E. Smith not out	14	) did not bat	
L. Jackson did not bat		)	
Extras	18	Extras	5
Total (for 8 wkts dec)	351	Total (for 5 wkts dec)	224

YORKSHIRE

First Innings		Second Innings	
W.B. Stott c Johnson b Buxton	42	Did not bat	
K. Taylor c Carr b Buxton	24	c Kelly b Smith	144
D.E.V. Padgett b Buxton	4	b Buxton	44
P.J. Sharpe b Smith	37	b Smith	42
H.D. Bird c Lee b Smith	1	not out	1
R. Illingworth c Kelly b Morgan	28	not out	47
J. Birkenshaw c Dawkes b Jackson	25	Did not bat	
J.R. Burnet b Smith	4	c Hamer b Smith	12
J.G. Binks b Richardson	15	)	
R.K. Platt not out	57	) did not bat	
C. Wood c Smith b Carr	10	)	
Extras	24	Extras	14
Total	275	Total (for 4 wkts)	304

Bowling

DERBYSHIRE (first innings): Platt 28-7-65-2; Wood 18-1-48-0; Taylor 15-4-43-0; Illingworth 30-6-74-4; Birkenshaw 36-8-103-1; (second innings): Platt 11-3-37-1; Wood 4-0-21-0; Illingworth 23-3-78-1; Birkenshaw 19-4-69-1; Taylor 3-0-13-0; Padgett 1-0-1-0.
YORKSHIRE (first innings): Jackson 27-7-53-1; Richardson 16-2-53-1; Buxton 20-6-50-3; Morgan 21-13-33-1; Carr 3.5-0-11-1. (second innings): Jackson 12-1-58-0; Richardson 4-0-23-0; Morgan 17-0-77-0; Smith 14.5-0-77-3; Carr 5-0-29-0; Buxton 4-0-26-1.

2

Brian Bolus

Gloucestershire v Yorkshire
Bristol 1959
22nd, 24th, 25th August

JOHN BRIAN BOLUS, *born 31.1.1934, Whitkirk (Leeds). Right-hand opening or middle-order batsman, left-arm medium-pace bowler. Played 107 matches for Yorkshire between 1956 and 1962 before moving to Notts where he was capped by England in 1963 and toured India in 1963-64. Captained Notts in 1972, then joined Derbyshire as captain 1973-75. Won a county cap with all three first-class counties. Lives in Notts and is a member of the Notts CCC Committee.*

Yorkshire's "southern tour" of between two and five matches usually came towards the end of the season and preceded the Scarborough Festival. The last day's county cricket to be seen in the 1959 season by the long-suffering Yorkshire public had been at Headingley on 11th August when Kent had been beaten by two wickets. Yorkshire came from a long way behind to win this game with Brian Close (despite his protests that he was not fit to play, let alone bowl) taking eight second-innings wickets for 41 – his career-best performance!

Thus we set out on the final five-match tour as one of four counties in with a chance of taking the championship in what Wisden described as "one of the most thrilling fights for a long time". We beat Middlesex at Lord's and then lost to Somerset at Bath. Now we had games against Gloucs, Worcs and Sussex to play ... and so we arrived in Bristol on the evening of 21st August ...

On the next, bright and sunny, Saturday morning Gloucs won the toss and elected to bat. Trueman and Illingworth were away playing for England v India so our opening attack was Bob Platt and Brian Close who swung the ball and seamed it on a wicket of modest pace and bounce but were unable to manage much penetration. Ken Taylor was the first change, followed by the two young and inexperienced spinners, Don Wilson and Jackie Birkenshaw. Nevertheless only Tom Graveney of the Gloucs batsmen had managed any sort of substantial score (67). Then, at No.6 in the order, came John Mortimore who, ironically, had just been dropped from the England team in favour of his Gloucs team-mate and fellow off-spinner, David Allen (who was left out of the Test XI). Mortimer now proceeded to make a crucial contribution of 76. In the final session only one wicket fell and we were unable to separate the ninth-wicket pair of David Smith and Barrie Meyer who then put on 71. The day ended with Gloucs 294 for eight. Yorkshire had bowled 128 overs in the day of which Close's share was 42.

In those far-off days Sunday was a day of rest for county cricketers which could be used when necessary to recover from six successive days of cricket plus the excesses of Saturday night, usually referred to in the Yorkshire camp as "Amami Night".

Accordingly, after a couple of drinks with the Gloucs team and taking advice on a suitable local hostelry for the Saturday night revels, we descended on The Rummer Bar, in the city centre and not far from our hotel. The Rummer Bar was one of the first of the steak-bars now springing up around the West Country and a good steak was not too often to be found in 1959. Don't forget food rationing had only ended five years earlier.

The Rummer Bar, however, also specialised in serving copious glasses of sherry – like the steaks, excellent value for money – which was dispensed in glasses of various sizes, the largest being the schooner. I don't know whether these had any historical connection with sea-faring matters but they were most certainly responsible for sinking the good ship Yorkshire that night. Brian Close showed early and unmistakable signs of leadership which were in time to distinguish him as captain of Yorkshire and England. All went well, and reasonably quietly, for a time until Close was challenged by our 12th man, Barry Stead, to a drinking contest involving the afore-mentioned schooners.

At this point, Ronnie Burnet, captain of Yorkshire and a man of wisdom and discretion, upped and left. He was followed, at intervals, by the more sensible souls until all that was left was a rabble (or was it a rump?) who were neither wise nor discreet. This included me. Eventually, the most difficult time arrived when we had to negotiate a reasonably decorous passage to the sanctuary of our hotel rooms. Certain heroics were observed on this journey. Don Wilson, for instance, accomplished it on hands and knees, clearly influenced by the work of his father for the Craven Pothole Rescue team!

Worse was to follow for those who reached the hotel. They may have thought the lights in the foyer offered the sort of haven extended by the harbour-lights of old Aberdeen, or perhaps Whitby, but it was not so.

We now found Bob Platt engaged in a desperate damage-limitation exercise because the hotel's night-porter was seriously disposed to telephone the police to deal with the worse-for-wear cricketers now occupying his forecourt. Mr. Platt (known to us as The Major because of his stately bearing and classy dress-sense) could normally be relied upon to give a splendid impression of righteous indignation, but now began to falter in his performance. Self-control is difficult when half-crazed by the demon drink.

The argument was ranging into the higher octaves when George Alcock, physiotherapist, was awakened in his lair. While showing due respect to the senior players, George regarded himself as the guardian of the physical and spiritual welfare of the younger ones. (He had also

Chris Old played a part in the late 1960s and became a regular in the 1970s. (Photo by George P. Herringshaw)

the hardest and most penetrative fingers I have ever known – a certain advantage in the days before we had much medical machinery!) He also had a sense of humour but this was not one of the moments when it was in evidence. Descending the stairs and observing the carnage, his wrath knew no bounds. He targeted young Birkenshaw and wanted to see him packed off home to Rothwell at once! This so unhinged Dickie Bird that he embarked on an impersonation of the comedian

Harry Worth which has continued over the later years and ultimately resulted in his becoming a first-class umpire.

It was the following morning before calm was totally restored – by Ronnie Burnet, who smoothed things over with a marvellous imperturbability. The team spent the remainder of the day in suffering/ reflection/regret/recovery. And while this was going on a strange meteorological phenomenon occurred. Thick fog settled over Bristol and much of the Severn estuary. With temperatures remaining at summer levels the pitch "sweated". On Monday morning, arriving at the ground, we found that not only had we a green pitch to bat on but the fog still hung like a pall over the ground. We couldn't see the roofs of the hospital buildings just outside the ground. And in these conditions, Gloucs declared at their Saturday night total and prepared to bowl at us.

Now Tony Brown (an assistant secretary at the TCCB but at that time Gloucs's opening bowler) does not quite recall the conditions as vividly as I have described them – but then he wouldn't, would he? Gloucs bowled us out for 35 in 21.5 overs and Tony recorded his career-best figures of seven for 11. I arrived at the crease at 22 for three and made 12 not out. There was one leg-bye and the next six batsmen all failed to score. Wisden records that "both medium-fast bowlers (Brown and David Smith) made the ball swing in the air and move disturbingly off the pitch". And while it would be fair to say we did not bat too well, the bowlers certainly exploited the conditions expertly.

Ronnie Burnet, reeling from this somewhat modest performance by his side, consulted the senior players and they reasoned that since "I had got my eye in" I should open the second innings as we followed on. The feeling was that because the light was so bad, only someone who had been recently batting for some time had any chance of seeing the ball properly. Dickie Bird, in his later umpiring career, wouldn't have allowed *any* play at all in that light. This rather novel piece of thinking proved successful for me, at least. But sadly, approaching what would have been my maiden first-class hundred, I went to pull Tony Brown, missed and was lbw for 91. Perhaps I should have known better. During the course of my innings I had been given this advice by one of the umpires, Dai Davies (612 games for Glamorgan): "Whatever you do, boy, don't hook or pull at Bristol." This was delivered in those soft, languid Welsh cadences – and I hadn't heeded the advice.

Our second innings was played out in sunshine and conditions eased as the pitch dried but we had been undone by those fateful 75 minutes in the morning. At close of play we were 141 for seven. Ronnie Burnet, not out and off the mark, was thus one of those first-innings batsmen who had failed to score but who had now avoided his "pair". However, as captain he was incensed by Press reports in Monday evening's newspapers that "it had been a totally irresponsible performance by Yorkshire." He insisted that freak atmospheric conditions plus bad light had been the main cause of the debacle. To drive his point home, he told the reporters: "You all know I am no longer a very good batsman but I'll tell you this: If it's sunny tomorrow, Gloucs won't get me out on that pitch."

And he certainly proved that point – 22 not out when the game ended.

Only the last act of this drama now remained to be played out. The remaining batsmen would all try to delay the almost-certain defeat for as long as possible and at the same time avoid their "pairs". However, should Bob Platt arrive at the wicket while the game was still beyond salvation, he was to be run out, 0, if necessary so that he *did* bag a pair. Bob took his batting very seriously indeed; we had all been assured of this on more than one occasion! In fact one has to say that he was always impeccably turned out and had a genuinely skilful and effective technique against spin bowling. Facing anything quicker than Mother Shipton, however, it was a different matter . . .

At 175 for nine we were still 64 runs short and Bob arrived at the crease. He took guard, looked imperiously round the field and prepared to receive the bowling. But at the first opportunity and frantic to get off the mark and avoid *his* pair, he played the ball towards cover and called his captain for a run. Ronnie let him get half-way, then sent him back! Cover picked up the ball and shied at Bob's stumps. It was then that we saw Barrie Meyer, standing back, had not got up to the stumps to collect the ball. It went for four overthows and Robert Kenworthy Platt, batsman extraordinary, was off the mark.

Both sides erupted into fits of laughter, Gloucs out in the middle, Yorkshire in front of the dressing-room. The Major was apoplectic with fury at this levity. No one ever quite seemed to treat his batting with the respect he felt it deserved. Then he realised the overthrows were credited to him, of course. He had not bagged a pair.

Our innings closed at 182; we had lost by an innings and 77 runs by 12 noon on the third day. Now it was time for sober reflection on a disastrous defeat and what it might have meant to us. We drove the short distance to Worcester with just that game and Sussex at Hove to complete the 1959 season. Those two stories belong to someone else . . .

GLOUCESTERSHIRE

First Innings

D.M. Young c Bolus b Platt	20
C.A. Milton c Bolus b Platt	15
R.B. Nicholls lbw b Close	3
T.W. Graveney b Birkenshaw	67
D. Hawkins st Binks b Close	13
J, Mortimore c Binks b Taylor	76
A. Brown b Birkenshaw	1
D. Allen run out	16
D. Smith not out	49
B. Meyer not out	23
Extras	11
Total (for 8 wkts dec)	294

YORKSHIRE

First Innings		**Second Innings**	
W.B. Stott b Smith	1	b Smith	2
K. Taylor b Brown	7	b Brown	8
D.E.V. Padgett c Meyer b Brown	4	hit wkt b Allen	12
D.B. Close lbw b Smith	3	b Mortimore	1
J.B. Bolus not out	12	lbw b Brown	91
H.D. Bird b Brown	0	run out	5
J. Birkenshaw b Brown	0	b Smith	10
D. Wilson b Smith	0	c Nicholls b Smith	9
J.G. Binks c Meyer b Brown	0	b Smith	11
J.R. Burnet b Brown	0	not out	22
R.K. Platt b Brown	0	b Brown	4
Extras	8	Extras	7
Total	35	Total	182

Bowling
GLOUCESTERSHIRE: Platt 29-10-59-2; Close 42-10-115-2; Taylor 18-7-26-1; Wilson 21-8-34-0; Birkenshaw 18-4-49-2.
YORKSHIRE (first innings): Smith 11-3-16-3; Brown 10.5-5-11-7; (second innings): Smith 35-5-68-4; Brown 27.5-11-54-3; Mortimore 28-17-19-1; C. Cook 5-0-15-0; Allen 16-7-19-1.

3

Bryan Stott

Worcestershire v Yorkshire
Worcester 1959
26th, 27th, 28th August

W ILLIAM BRYAN STOTT, *born 18.7.1934, Yeadon. Left-hand bat, occasional off-break bowler, good fieldsman. Played 187 matches for Yorkshire between 1952-63, scored 1,000 runs in a season five times and 2,034 in 1959 when he played a dramatic role in the winning of the championship at Hove. Had to retire prematurely to help with the family plumbing business of which he is now a director. A member of the Yorkshire CCC Committee.*

The 1959 match at Hove was in so many ways momentous and we all, I am sure, have personal memories of the game. It is right that the captain should describe the occasion himself but perhaps I may help to set the scene, to put the final game in context?

It had not been a particularly brilliant first half of the season. We had beaten Notts, Glamorgan, Hampshire, Warwickshire and Essex but we had lost to Lancashire, Surrey (twice) and Hampshire (away) and, not enjoying a lot of luck with the weather, we had drawn seven matches when we embarked on the final southern tour of five games. Surrey and Gloucestershire were in close contention for the title and, after winning it for the past seven years, Surrey were not going to surrender it lightly. They had, as we have seen, beaten us twice, at The Oval and at Park Avenue that season. And Gloucestershire, with strong batting and a nicely-balanced attack, were having a particularly good season.

Nevertheless, we were certainly not prepared for the events at Bristol in the previous game (described by Brian Bolus); it was a shattering blow to our hopes and made it absolutely essential that we win at Worcester to have any interest in the title. The game in Bristol was finished by noon on the third day and over lunch I said that I was going to Droitwich (before booking in at our hotel in Worcester) to take a brine-bath. My legs were aching badly and that seemed to me to be the best way of easing the problem.

Several of the lads took up the idea and then at Worcester we were rejoined by Fred and Illy who had been on Test duty at The Oval while we were being hammered in Bristol. That was obviously going to make a difference; Dickie Bird and Jackie Birkenshaw dropped out of the side to make way for them.

Obviously it was nice to carry my bat through the innings; naturally I was pleased about it. But I don't want to dwell on that. What was most gratifying about the six-wickets win in Worcester was the really professional job we did as a team. It had not been the best start to a season we had ever had because Ronnie (Burnet) was unlucky enough to lose the toss 13 times running and we usually found it difficult to get into a position where we could dictate the course of a·game.

The turning-point, I think, came at Chesterfield where Don Carr's declaration opened the door just wide enough to give a chance to win. Even so, we had to make over 300 in the fourth innings and Ken Taylor got a marvellous 144 in quick time. I must not, of course, forget the contribution of Platt, already described in loving detail.

It was a good win and it was followed up by another at Scarborough. Nevertheless, there had been set-backs against Surrey and Northants,

Barry Leadbeater, who made his debut in 1966. (Photo by Telegraph & Argus, Bradford)

and then the disaster at Bristol. At Worcester, it all came right. Everyone seemed to chip in with a positive contribution whether it was runs, wickets or in the field. Ronnie would be the first, I am sure, to say he got sound information from Closey and the important thing was, he *listened* to it. The input from Illingworth and Binks was of tremendous value and we were on the way to becoming a thoroughly professional outfit. That was completed a bit later, but we were certainly on the way and it showed throughout the whole game at Worcester.

They held us up for a long time in their second innings – after being 142 behind in the first; that was precisely what they had to do. But in the Yorkshire camp everyone worked ... and kept on working.

It set up the position for the grandstand finish at Hove in the next game. But, as I see it, that was the time we grew up as a team. Up to the last few games of the 1959 season we had been a bunch of chaps earning a living in a rather pleasant way. We then became an efficient and professional outfit and we got better all the time. To come back from the disaster at Bristol to win the next two games by sheer hard work and application marked us as something a bit better than average. I like to think Yorkshire stayed that way for the next decade, at least.

WORCESTERSHIRE

First Innings		Second Innings	
M.J. Horton b Platt	1	b Trueman	51
R.G.A. Headley c Bolus b Close	36	lbw b Close	28
A. Spencer c Bolus b Close	10	c Binks b Trueman	39
D. Kenyon c Taylor b Close	7	c Binks b Close	122
D.W. Richardson c Binks b Trueman	16	not out	36
R.G. Broadbent c Close b Illingworth	1	st Binks b Close	0
R. Booth b Close	9	b Illingworth	4
L. Coldwell c Taylor b Illingworth	4	c Padgett b Illingworth	0
D.B. Pearson not out	27	c Stott b Close	1
K.J. Aldridge b Trueman	8	b Trueman	1
D. Pratt b Trueman	0	b Trueman	0
Extras	1	Extras	19
Total	120	Total	301

YORKSHIRE

First Innings		Second Innings	
W.B. Stott not out	144	lbw b Coldwell	21
K. Taylor c Broadbent b Coldwell	9	c Spencer b Aldridge	0
D.E.V. Padgett c and b Pratt	48	lbw b Pratt	32
D.B. Close b Coldwell	19	c Spencer b Aldridge	26
R. Illingworth c Broadbent b Aldridge	2	not out	40
J.B. Bolus b Coldwell	1	not out	37
D. Wilson c Broadbent b Aldridge	11	)	
J.R. Burnet lbw b Pearson	14	)	
F.S. Trueman b Coldwell	2	) did not bat	
J.G. Binks b Coldwell	0	)	
R.K. Platt c Broadbent b Coldwell	0	)	
Extras	12	Extras	7
Total	262	Total (for 4 wkts)	163

Bowling

WORCESTERSHIRE (first innings): Trueman 12.4-4-37-3; Platt 9-3-19-1; Close 16-4-34-4; Taylor 3-2-8-0; Illingworth 10-3-21-2; (second innings): Trueman 24.5-6-58-4; Platt 16-4-55-0; Illingworth 31-13-46-2; Close 31-11-99-4; Wilson 15-7-22-0; Taylor 2-0-2-0.

YORKSHIRE (first innings): Coldwell 29.1-9-66-6; Aldridge 17-5-52-2; Pearson 15-3-45-1; Horton 19-6-45-0; Pratt 19-2-42-1; (second innings): Coldwell 19-2-67-1; Aldridge 12-2-35-2; Horton 9-2-25-0; Pratt 9-2-29-1.

4

Ronnie Burnet

Sussex v Yorkshire
Hove 1959
29th, 30th August, 1st September

JOHN RONALD BURNET, born 11.10.1918. Saltaire. Right-hand batsman whose two years of captaincy, 1958 and 1959, saw the renaissance of Yorkshire cricket after seven years of Surrey dominance in the county championship. His leadership is dealt with in more detail in the introductory chapter of this book but undoubtedly it played a major part, when he was invited to move from Bradford League cricket to the first-class game at the age of 39, in the change of fortunes. He played in only 54 matches and scored 897 runs (seven catches and one wicket) but that is a largely irrelevant detail in a significant career.

Before describing what happened in this particular match – one of the most remarkable I have ever seen (never mind taken part in) – it is necessary to look at a few previous games. All of them had a tremendous influence on this, the final match of our 1959 season.

Having beaten Kent at Headingley a most extraordinary game, we started our southern tour, at that time the traditional ending to every season, by beating Middlesex at Lord's. This put us in a very favourable position to win the county championship and we went to Bath to play Somerset in a confident mood.

Now Brian Close (in spite of what has been written since that time, much of it by himself) was not, in fact, very forthcoming with advice in either 1958 or 1959. Suddenly, in the dressing-room at Bath, he announced, "If we act right in our heads we can win this championship." To this he received the response from one and all, "That's what *we* have been telling *you* for weeks." Fired by his new enthusiasm, Closey went on to advise, when we had to face Brian Langford on a crumbling pitch: "The only way to play him is to employ the sweep."

Now it might be a touch uncharitable to recall one or two occasions when Closey himself had employed the sweep with a spectacular lack of success! The fact was that up to that time the only first-class player to play the shot with any degree of consistent success had been Denis Compton. As a "business" stroke, the sweep was virtually unknown, unlike today. So Closey gave us all a demonstration, there and then in the dressing-room, on how to execute it… the art of sweeping.

We needed to score 254 on this (as I say) crumbling pitch and three of us (including, I am ashamed to say, myself) were bowled while sweeping, and we lost by 16 runs. Quite simply we had not mastered the basic requirement – first of all make sure that your front pad is in line with the ball! I am convinced, to this day, that if we had batted in an orthodox manner we would have won. It would have solved a few of our problems. As things were, it proved a major set-back to our challenge. And so we went on to Bristol to play Gloucs who were also challenging for the title.

We then met the most amazing atmospheric conditions I have ever seen in any kind of cricket and were bowled out on the Monday morning for 35 runs. The temperature was in the 80s and it was like playing in a huge ballroom with a blue-grey ceiling 15 feet above our heads! The light (as someone else has said) would have prevented Dickie Bird, in his modern role of umpire, from allowing anyone out of the pavilion.

So two losses in two games put our whole season in jeopardy as we travelled to Worcester for the penultimate game. And here, all looked lost when, in the middle of the last afternoon, Worcs were 274 for three with Don Kenyon in full flow. It was then that Brian Close *did* come into his own with the inspired advice of a double change in the bowling. The result was that Worcs lost their last seven wickets for 27 runs to be all out for 301. This left us to score 163 against the clock and from the slightly dodgy position of 87-4, Ray Illingworth and Brian Bolus saw us home with 40 not out and 37 not out respectively.

Naturally, we went to Hove in better heart, especially as the other challengers had faltered. We were still in with a good chance. However, the heatwave was unrelenting and with a combination of continual blazing sunshine and grounds as hard as concrete, several of us were looking a bit weary. One final effort had now to be made, nevertheless. And what a match it turned out to be!

I won't dwell too long on the first two days as all the drama, naturally, occurred on the last one. We started well enough, getting Sussex in trouble at 67-6. Ken Taylor, as first change, bowled superbly, taking four of the first five wickets and finishing with 4-40 from 22 overs. Then Don Smith and "Tiger" Pataudi stopped the rot, scoring 49 and 52 respectively, and Sussex recovered to 210 all out. Curiously enough, our first innings was remarkably similar – Bolus 1, Padgett 0, Close 14, Taylor 3. Bryan Stott had stayed resolutely at one end until joined by Illingworth and this pair steadied the ship. Then Stott was caught and bowled but Raymond, who had grown up very rapidly in his whole attitude into a true professional, batted superbly, ably supported by, first, Jackie Birkenshaw with 38 and then a big-hitting innings of 55 by Don Wilson. Illingworth went on to reach 122 before being caught behind but we had a lead of 97.

Sussex batted more solidly the second time round and soon knocked off the arrears for the loss of two wickets. They went through the second day and into the last when there was a 4.30 pm finish, including the extra half-hour. We were, quite frankly, in a desperate situation at lunch because even if they had declared then, we would have needed to score at about 100 an hour. And their captain, Robin

*Brian Langford is bowled by Fred Trueman, Philip Sharpe looks on. MCC v Yorkshire
at Lord's in 1961. (Photo by S&G Press Agency)*

Marlar, made it absolutely clear that under no circumstances was he
going to declare since the championship was at stake. This had the
whole Yorkshire team seething, especially as news came through that
Middlesex were beating Surrey and Gloucs were also in trouble. If we
could win that one, we would probably take the championship.

But how were we going to do it? Freddie Trueman was, in his own
graphic terms, "knackered" and could achieve no penetration. It was
left to the spinners, Wilson and Illingworth, to winkle out the opposition. Pataudi was still there and now Ian Thomson was sticking. It
took nearly 40 more minutes to get the last three wickets and it was
started – let's give him all credit – by Thomson saying, "This is
bloody ridiculous," and having a big wa-hoo, to be bowled. Pataudi
followed and to the delight of everyone in our ranks, Marlar fell, first
ball, to a catch on the square leg boundary by Jackie Birkenshaw. In
fact one of my better memories of that whole innings is of seeing
Jackie, with his fresh, schoolboy appearance, nonchalantly taking
four catches in that position. He didn't have to move his feet. He took
the catches without any fuss, no throwing the ball into the air. And
nobody kissed him!

Just the same, we had now to reflect that our task was virtually impossible. We had to score 218 runs in a maximum of 107 minutes and obviously Sussex were going to do everything they possibly could to prevent it. We were "mad" and frustrated. We had not even been given the ghost of a chance. I said, "Look, lads. If you want to show up Marlar for what we think he is, we can do a go-slow and the job's finished. Or... we can do as we've done all season and give it a go although we really haven't a chance."

Then I wrote out the batting-order: Stott, Close, Taylor at No.3 and moved Padgett down to No.4. This caused a furore in the dressing-room, especially from the two senior players, Closey and Freddie, who said, "If you put Padgie at No.4 we've lost already," to which I replied, "While you buggers are having a big wa-hoo, Padgett will score off every ball." I hadn't set out the order without a lot of thought and I stuck to my guns. It was one of the best decisions I ever made...

To say that the start of the innings was dramatic is a big under-statement: after the first over we were 12! Before he was out, Close scored a quick dozen but even that gave us some problems. He hit a six so far over the scoreboard that it took nearly three minutes to get the ball back. And we couldn't afford to lose three minutes. After 19 minutes we were 52 and that time included the dismissal of two batsmen and men going out to replace them. And I think the batsmen crossed *on the pitch*, never mind the ground! Bryan Stott had scored 37 of the 52 in glorious style and it was then that Doug Padgett joined him.

The next hour brought one of the most wonderful displays of batsmanship I have seen, before or since. Marlar had seven men posted on the boundary and to counter this Stott and Padgett played what I can only describe as "tip and run." So good was their running between the wickets that they were taking two off nearly every ball. When Marlar brought men in to stem this flow they crashed the ball through to the boundary... exactly, it seemed, to the place just vacated by the fielder who had been brought in! It was wonderful batting. It ended when Thomson bowled Padgett for 79. He and Stott had put on 141 in exactly an hour, against defensive fields. And Padgett (who, according to the prophets, was going to lose the match for us if he went in at No. 4) had actually made up 37 runs on Stott since he went in!

That quite magnificent partnership meant that we had scored 193 in 79 minutes. We could now stroll to victory in round about a mere run a minute! I made no further changes in the batting order and Brian Bolus saw us home with a glance to fine leg for the winning run. We had scored 218 off 28 overs and three balls. We were the champions.

Ironically, in reaching that impossible target, we had proved Marlar right in refusing to declare although I still feel that if he had set us a difficult but not unreasonable target we might have struggled. As it was, the lads were hopping mad and really fired up. One episode during our innings did nothing to cool our tempers. At a crucial point in our innings, Tiger Pataudi took a magnificent catch on the boundary edge – but he had put one foot a few inches over the line. Sportsman and gentleman that he was, he held up both hands to indicate a six-hit, whereupon his captain ran across and, as we all saw it, "gave him a mouthful" for not claiming the catch. That *really* got the lads going.

I don't think I have ever seen such scenes in a dressing-room as those at the end of the match. There was a somewhat uncharitable, perhaps, attitude of "We've done the bastards," although no one was actually specific about who "the bastards" were. It was, I suppose, inevitable. Nobody ever *gave* Yorkshire *anything*. Then, euphoria took over. The Sussex team joined us in the celebrations and their secretary, bless his heart, produced a case of champagne from nowhere. We certainly hadn't ordered it. We wouldn't have dared to, and perhaps have to pay for it for without cause for celebration! The dressing-room filled up with genuine supporters, neutral well-wishers and, indeed, anybody else who could convince us that he or she had a right to be there. I had to go out and address a large crowd that had gathered and then go to the top of the stand to be interviewed by Robert Hudson who had managed – just – to keep up with our progress in a continuous radio broadcast to the nation. This had resulted, we learned later, in work stopping all over Yorkshire!

Then came a telephone call from ITV asking me to appear with Huw Thomas on News at Ten. It was then that I suggested to Padgett, my usual passenger, that he get a lift with someone else as far as the Bell Inn at Eaton Socon, on the A1 near Bedford, and I would catch up with the lads there. Alf and Jenny, who kept The Bell, were special people and we always called there, going down or coming back from the south. It turned out to be one of the loneliest nights of my life...

By the time I had been feted and then interviewed by Huw Thomas (and don't forget it was a bit of a special celebration for a lot of people after Surrey's seven-year domination) it was rather late. Putting my foot down hard in my Jaguar R.B. 3.4 I managed to reach The Bell in 55 minutes – but it was now 11.20 pm. The news which greeted me was that most of the team had departed 20 minutes earlier. I was so tired and hungry that I stayed to have one of Jenny's wonderful steaks with all the trimmings and shared with my hosts a bottle of beautiful Burgundy.

I then set off to re-join the boys in Scarborough but I was destined not to make it. I seemed to wake up with a start just north of

Doncaster and realised to my horror that the last thing I could remember was driving into Bawtry! It was a frightening realisation and I immediately decided that by opening the windows and playing loud music on the radio I might just make it through Wakefield and Bradford to my home in Baildon. I did. But my family were then at the Balmoral Hotel in Scarborough! So I telephoned at 3am in the morning to report that I was alive and well and staying the night in Baildon. In the background, I could hear a fantastic party going on. I dropped into my bed and slept the sleep of the just.

At 8.30 the following morning I set off again for Scarborough and met with the reception committee which had such a profound effect on Jackie Birkenshaw (see his chapter). The ground was packed. Someone carried my bag to the dressing-room and I got the sort of cheer that greeted all the boys, individually, as they went into the ground. Such was the enthusiasm of the success-starved Yorkshire supporters that when a team photograph as taken as we went out, the Pavilion clock showed that it was well after the time we should have been in action.

Some might say that it was appropriate to have in our dressing-room in Hove, at the moment of victory, Harry Secombe, who had been a good friend during our visit. At that time he was known less as a singer and more as a member of the celebrated Goons. It was sad, I thought, that many older players (some, unfortunately, from our own county) suggested that *we* were a set of Goons and had been extremely lucky to win the championship. But we hadn't, you know. We had lost seven matches, and I have known Yorkshire to lose fewer than that and finish third from the bottom of the table. BUT (and it's a big but) we had won 14 games with only one declaration offered us, and that of dubious generosity by Donald Carr of Derbyshire, who batted on for ten minutes after lunch and set us 304 in 175 minutes. We did that with time to spare. In all other matches we had to bowl out the opposition before we could think about winning and this, remember, was in three-day games, not four. We regularly bowled over 100 overs in a day.

Without doubt it was a turning point in Yorkshire cricket history. At the pre-season lunch, Brian Sellers, the cricket chairman, had said that "we were in the process of re-building and could not expect to win the championship in the next three or four years." This did, in fact, have an unforeseen effect on the team. After winning the Minor Counties championship in 1957 the younger players felt they now ought to win the County Championship as of right. And their attitude rubbed off on some of the older players.

If I did anything useful in 1958-59 I like to think that the change in attitude of the older and more established players in the side was decisive. In some cases suddenly (and in others gradually) they realised that cricket was a game they could actually enjoy, even though it was a deadly serious matter and we were always going out for a win. I am quite sure that this change of attitude rescued the international careers of Close and Trueman and that Illingworth was completely on the right track, as he was later to prove.

Be that as it may, certainly that new spirit was to make Yorkshire the most respected and most successful side of the 1960s. It was a spirit which prevailed until the disastrous 1970s, from which Yorkshire have not yet recovered and will not do so until that spirit once again pervades the whole club. I cannot believe that the answer lies in overseas players and certainly *not* in non-Yorkshiremen from other counties.

SUSSEX

First Innings		Second Innings	
A.S.M. Oakman st Binks b Taylor	33	b Close	7
L.S. Lenham c Taylor b Trueman	4	c Stott b Wilson D	66
K.G. Suttle c Illingworth b Taylor	5	st Binks b Wilson D	22
E.R. Dexter c and b Taylor	14	c Birkenshaw b Wilson D	33
J.M. Parks c Bolus b Taylor	6	c Birkenshaw b Wilson D	85
G.H.G. Doggart lbw b Close	5	c Birkenshaw b Illingworth	10
D.V. Smith c Close b Illingworth	49	c Bolus b Taylor	31
Nawab of Pataudi b Trueman	52	c Close b Illingworth	37
N.I.Thomson lbw b Illingworth	21	b Illingworth	12
A.E James b Illingworth	4	not out	0
R.G. Marlar not out	13	c Birkenshaw b Illingworth	0
Extras	4	Extras	8
Total	210	Total	311

YORKSHIRE

First Innings		Second Innings	
W.B. Stott c and b Suttle	34	c N. of Pataudi b Marlar	96
B. Bolus hit wkt b Dexter	1	not out	6
D.E.V. Padgett c Parks b Dexter	0	b Thomson	79
D.B. Close b Dexter	14	c Parks b Dexter	12
R. Illingworth c Parks b James	122	not out	5
K. Taylor lbw b Thomson	3	lbw b Dexter	1
J. Birkenshaw lbw b Marlar	38	)	
D. Wilson c Oakman b Marlar	55	) Did not bat	
J.R. Burnet c Marlar b Dexter	1	)	
F.S. Trueman c N. of Pataudi b James	7	st Parks, b Marlar	11
J. G. Binks not out	1	Did not bat	
Extras	31	Extras	8
Total	307	Total (5 wkts)	218

Bowling

SUSSEX (first innings): Trueman 19-5-40-2; Close 17-5-54-1; Taylor 22-9-40-4; Illingworth 14.2-3-51-3; Wilson 5-1-21-0; (second innings): Trueman 24-5-60-0; Close 19-6-51-1; Illingworth 28.3-8-66-4; Taylor 8-5-5-1; Birkenshaw 7-0-43-0; Wilson 24-7-78-4.

YORKSHIRE (first innings): Thomson 31-7-65-1; Dexter 29-7-63-4; Smith 4-1-14-0; James 24-4-67-2; Marlar 15.4-7-29-2; Suttle 6-1-20-0; Oakman 6-1-18-0; Doggart 1-1-0-0; (second innings): Thomson 10-0-87-1; Dexter 10.3-0-69-2; James 2-0-15-0; Marlar 6-0-39-2.

5

Philip Sharpe

Sussex v Yorkshire
Hove 1959 (another view)
29th, 30th August, 1st September 1959

PHILIP JOHN SHARPE, *born 27.12.1936, Baildon. Right-hand bat, occasional off-break bowler, outstanding slip fieldsman (71 catches in 1962, 617 in his career). Played 411 matches for Yorkshire between 1958 and 1974, scoring 1,000 runs in a season 12 times and 2,252 in 1962. Later played for Derbyshire and Norfolk. Twelve Tests, averaging 46.23 (17 catches). Now a member of the Yorkshire CCC Committee.*

The year 1959 had not, so far, gone well for me. I was not yet a capped player; I had scraped together around 600 runs without making a century either as an opening batsman or at four, five and six in the order. And, quite rightly, I had been dropped from the side. I would not be making the final tour of the south and west.

Earlier in the season, however, my father had arranged a business trip to coincide with the Worcester match so it seemed entirely the logical thing to do to accompany him and support the lads with whom I had already spent a large part of the summer. Obviously I arrived at an opportune moment because George Alcock, the physiotherapist, had just told Ronnie Burnet that Cyril Turner (the pre-war all-rounder and now Yorkshire's scorer) was not well and ought to return home. Who was to do the scoring?

Duggie Padgett suggested me! This was received by one and all with what seemed unnecessary enthusiasm, but... well... I might as well support the team from the scorebox as anywhere else. So I sharpened a few pencils and took up my post. It was (as Bryan Stott describes) a good win and it opened up all sorts of possibilities at Hove. There was also the little matter of the players' end-of-season party to be considered and, being as sociable as the next man, I didn't really want to miss it. So I drove over to Sussex with Don Wilson and once again watched from the sidelines while my father returned home.

It was on the social front that the first problem arose in sunny Brighton. The *Daily Express* (thanks very much!) carried a front-page story to the effect that Yorkshire wives had put the block on our end-of-term festivities, scheduled for that Saturday night. These were due to take the normal form which meant we needed a few dancing partners and that usually fell within the province of George Alcock who was despatched to the neighbouring nurses' homes to round up a few volunteers.

The *Express* story, however, was seen as not entirely helpful. The wives (back home in Yorkshire) who had read it, and even those who hadn't, now kept the telephone lines busy with inquiries which might have seemed pertinent to them but were just a trifle irrelevant to the warriors assembled on the south coast. There was to be no trawling of the nurses' homes and any dancing we had in mind was to be with each other. We looked around the hotel and no-one seemed to fancy the choice of partners now available.

But fortune usually smiles on the righteous and it was a chance visit to the Hippodrome Theatre by F.S. Trueman and R.K. Platt which solved our problems. They had really gone to see, and have a chat with, Harry Secombe, the star of the show, but they returned with a line of chorus girls. The party was a success and I seem to remember spending the Sunday-off (no limited-overs thrash to bother us in those days) rather pleasantly with a new girl-friend.

There was still work to be done, just the same, by scorers no less than players. I had "had a net" as it were, at Worcester, in the statistician's role but I regret to say it had not prepared me for the duties as they needed to be performed on the last afternoon. The Sussex scorer – I can remember him only as "George" – was, mercifully, a benign and understanding chap who did nothing more than smile indulgently at his colleague's somewhat eccentric behaviour. I was on my feet throughout the whole of the Yorkshire second innings . . . never sat down once!

I don't know how Cyril Turner would have coped with the situation, or Ted Lester in later years; they had both played many times for

Brian Crump snicks a ball from Ray Illingworth past Philip Sharpe and Jimmy Binks, MCC v Yorkshire at Lord's in 1961. (Photo by S&G Press Agency)

Yorkshire and I'm sure they wouldn't have got through without the stirring of a few patriotic instincts. Perhaps they might have expressed them differently. But I was 22 years old and I felt very much a part of that Yorkshire team. The championship depended on our winning the game and – there was no help for it – I was *involved*.

It was a day of many calculations. At first it seemed laboured and drawn-out. With the championship hanging on the result, we couldn't expect any quixotic declaration. It was one of those days when the opposition had to be *winkled out*, somehow. It was a morning when Illingworth and Wilson were going to have a lot of bowling to do because Sussex batted in depth. The Nawab of Pataudi – afterwards captain of India in 40 Tests – was actually at No.8 in the order. Above him, at No.7, was Don Smith who, two years earlier, had opened the batting in three Tests for England. And before that came a brilliant line-up of talent which included the prolific Dexter and Jim Parks, who averaged over 50 that season for Sussex.

Rumours went around about an argument in the Sussex camp during lunch over the declaration time, but none came. They batted on until well into the afternoon and play was due to finish at half-past four. At last Illingworth took the final wicket and any chance of a win seemed inconceivable. But the championship was at stake and Yorkshire hadn't been this close for a long, long time.

The chase was started by the left-handed Stott – who hit Ian Thomson's first ball straight back over his head for six! The rest of the story must be left to Ronnie Burnet but I can say that the Yorkshire scorer was never off his feet for one moment. The 50 was up in four overs before I had had a chance to write the bowlers' names in the scorebook. I can remember Closey *sweeping* Thomson over the score-board for six and even with seven men on the boundary, Robin Marlar couldn't stem the flow of runs. The running between the wickets of Stott and Padgett had to be seen to be believed.

Everyone batted in a way which was totally foreign to how we had been taught to play. But it was effective. The bowling figures must have haunted Thomson, Dexter, James and Marlar over the years. The target of 218 was reached in less than 100 minutes – off 28 overs and three balls. Yorkshire were champions . . . at last. Hove was a very good place for a Yorkshireman to be that afternoon.

And an after-thought: two young ladies from the show at the Hippodrome came that day to watch their first day of first-class cricket. If they ever watched any more it must have seemed a bit tame!

For scorecard see Ronnie Burnet chapter.

6

Jackie Birkenshaw

Yorkshire v MCC
Scarborough 1959
2nd, 3rd, 4th September

JACK BIRKENSHAW, *born 13.11.1940, Rothwell. Left-hand batsman, off-spin bowler. Played 30 times for Yorkshire between 1958 and 1960 before going to Leicestershire for the next 20 years during which he gained England selection. He had a brief spell with Worcestershire before turning to coaching. A versatile and popular cricketer, he once volunteered to open the batting when Yorkshire had injury problems – and did the job with a fair amount of success. He was appointed a first-class umpire in 1982, coached at Somerset and became cricket manager at Leicestershire in 1992.*

To select a match which was utterly meaningless as a competitive spectacle might, at first glance, seem rather eccentric – a match which started the Scarborough Festival of 1959. But it wasn't a matter of runs or wickets which was important; it was the atmosphere in the ground which made such an impression on me and which has remained in my mind ever since.

I was 18 years old at the time. I had played only a handful of games for the county side. I had just come back north, through the night, after the most dramatic and memorable game of cricket I had ever known. And in Scarborough I found a ground, already almost full more than an hour before the start, with the spectactors wanting to give every one of us a hero's welcome. Never, before or since, have I known anything like it.

About 18 hours previously Yorkshire had scored 218 in less than 29 overs to win not only the game against Sussex but the County Championship for the first time outright since 1946. That game is for Ronnie Burnet, the captain, to describe, but simply to be part of it was the most important part of my cricketing life up to that point. I had taken a good catch at deep extra cover to dismiss Jim Parks, played my part in a stand of 108 with Ray Illingworth and enjoyed learning a bit from watching him bowl. Illy was the best off-spinner when the pitch was "doing a bit" that I ever saw.

Then came the celebrations. Some Yorkshire supporters and committeemen had provided the champagne – the first my friend Don Wilson and I had ever drunk. We must have stayed a couple of hours in Hove after the game and there was still a drive of nearly 300 miles to be faced. But that wasn't my problem – I hadn't a car. So I was Illy's passenger as we drove to Scarborough ... with no motorways in 1959. It must have been 1am when we got to the Salisbury Hotel and I was *still* excited. Sleep, you might say, didn't come easily that night.

The next morning the celebrations started all over again because when we arrived at the ground we found several thousand Yorkshire men and women now wanted to join in. They applauded each and

Richard Hutton hits Hughes for four in his unbeaten 81 at Old Trafford against Lancashire in 1970. (Photo by B. Butterworth)

every one of us from the gates to the dressing-rooms; when we went out to field (and it wasn't a good toss to lose after the celebrations and the late bed-time) they formed a corridor almost the whole way to the middle and clapped us all the way.

It felt good to be alive and back home in Yorkshire. It was as if everyone in the crowd was anxious to be a part of the championship win. Indeed, I'm sure they all felt they *were* a part of it. Most of the game was played in an uproar of approval and when the spectactors were not cheering they were buzzing with the excitement of it. It was impossible not to get caught up in it all.

At least one small part of the game sticks in my mind. Now when you have bowled a few thousand overs in your time it might be thought difficult to single out one particular delivery but – believe me – I can remember one from that game. I rate it as the best single delivery I bowled in my entire life. It bit and it turned as Trevor Bailey tried to push it into the covers. It was difficult enough to *bowl* Trevor at the best of times and that was a belting pitch. I have never bowled a better ball.

It was a smashing game, too ... lots of runs scored and, once again, a thrilling chase for Yorkshire to win late on the third day. The only man who missed out in that chase was Dickie Bird, so often my team-mate in the Colts, later to be a colleague at Leicester. He was bowled by Harold Rhodes for none in what turned out to be his last game for Yorkshire. Poor old Dickie – but he's had his moments since.

We managed to please the crowd with a win and the party began all over again. There was just one more big day in that season – when Yorkshire went to The Oval the following week and beat a side representing the Rest of England. I was not part of that but I didn't mind too much. Hove followed by Scarborough was enough to keep one 18-year-old Yorkshire lad happy for a long, long time.

MCC

First Innings		Second Innings	
M.J. Horton c Stott b Illingworth	32	c Binks b Birkenshaw	80
P.E. Richardson lbw b Close	7	b Trueman	10
J.V. Wilson c Bolus b Wilson	7	b Illingworth	3
D.J. Insole c Binks b Birkenshaw	43	b Birkenshaw	56
T.E. Bailey b Birkenshaw	25	not out	37
A.C.D. Ingleby-Mackenzie			
b Birkenshaw	28	b Illingworth	50
P.J. Sainsbury run out	77	not out	15
R. Booth b Padgett	48	)	
R.V.C. Robins lbw b Bolus	22	) did not bat	
G.W. Richardson not out	30	)	
H.J. Rhodes not out	3	)	
Extras	7	Extras	10
Total (for 9 wkts dec)	329	Total (for 5 wkts dec)	261

YORKSHIRE

First Innings		Second Innings	
W.B. Stott c Booth b Bailey	83	run out	68
H.D. Bird c Insole b Bailey	58	b Rhodes	0
D.E.V. Padgett st Booth b Robins	10	c and b Sainsbury	58
D.B. Close b Bailey	0	not out	88
R. Illingworth not out	105	not out	35
J.B. Bolus lbw b Bailey	42		
J. Birkenshaw not out	23		
D. Wilson)			
J.R. Burnet) did not bat			
F.S. Trueman)			
J.G. Binks)			
Extras	10	Extras	11
Total (for 5 wkts dec)	331	Total (for 3 wkts)	260

Bowling
MCC (first innings): Trueman 12-0-45-0; Close 11-0-40-1; Wilson 35-6-142-1; Illingworth 16-4-29-1; Birkenshaw 13-3-28-3; Bolus 6-1-25-1; Padgett 5-1-13-1; (second innings): Trueman 18-1-78-1; Padgett 3-1-4-0; Illingworth 21-6-82-2; Wilson 8-0-57-0; Birkenshaw 11-2-30-2.
YORKSHIRE (first innings): Rhodes 20-2-89-0; Richardson 11-0-43-0; Bailey 22-4-60-4; Sainsbury 17-5-43-0; Horton 13-1-34-0; Robins 13-1-52-1; (second innings): Rhodes 12-0-57-1; Richardson 3-0-25-0; Bailey 10-3-55-0; Sainsbury 6-0-43-1; Robins 3-0-21-0; Horton 4-0-29-0; Ingleby-Mackenzie 1.4-0-13-0; Wilson 1-0-6-0.

7

Mel
Ryan

Lancashire v Yorkshire
Old Trafford 1960
30th July, 1st, 2nd August

MELVILLE RYAN, *born 23.6.1933, Huddersfield. Right-arm fast-medium bowler, right-hand lower order batsman. Played 150 matches for Yorkshire between 1954 and 1966, taking 413 wickets. Scored 682 runs and was one of that rare breed – a bowler who did not have an exaggerated opinion of his own batting! Keen golfer and shrewd business-man, is a partner in the family firm in Huddersfield.*

It was described at the time as "the county match of the century". One writer offered the view that it was the greatest Roses match ever. Over the three days of the August Bank Holiday weekend, 1960, a crowd of 74,000 watched this game. Television coverage was due to end and go over to other programmes long before it did – but stayed with the match until it finished off the very last ball of the extra half-hour.

And Yorkshire lost... bad enough in any championship game. Worse still, they lost to Lancashire. And no matter how the Roses match is said to have declined since the war, no matter how much it has changed character, to the players at any rate it has always been a very special occasion. Certainly it has to me. And even though I have to record a Lancashire victory, this one will always have a special place in my memories. No one left the ground on that last afternoon; no one could. It was edge-of-the-seat stuff such as few people have ever seen, and the tension affected every one of us out in the middle. Never mind the figures – the fact is that I bowled that Tuesday afternoon as if my very life depended on it. That's how I felt. But, as I say, the figures don't matter. This was Yorkshire cricket, fighting with backs to the wall, at its very best. The smallest blemish – a misfield or an ill-directed delivery – took on the proportions of a national disaster.

We started the Lancs second innings with little or no chance according to everyone except 11 Yorkshiremen but we attacked with everything we had got. Gradually we put Lancs behind the clock; then we pushed them *well* behind the clock. They were under the same pressure and wickets began to fall. I am absolutely certain that every fielder, apart from the bowlers and the batsmen, was drenched in sweat. The crowd must have been in the same state. They cheered, and they groaned; they applauded and they wrung their hands in anguish. They must have felt they were as much a part of the action as any player. It was an utterly unbelievable afternoon's cricket. And it had all started as a typical nothing-given, nothing-asked match between Lancashire and Yorkshire.

We scored a modest 154 with only Closey coming to terms with "George" Statham and Ken Higgs on a pitch which suited them.

Lancs replied with 226, a lead of 72, with most of the runs coming from the two left-handers Bob Barber and Alan Wharton.

The second innings was even worse with Statham taking another four and a couple of leg-spinners tormenting us so that we were all out for 149. And it was then that the fun really started: Lancashire needed only 78 to win and they had plenty of time – two hours and five minutes – to get them. We set out to make it as difficult as possible. Never since 1893 had Lancashire achieved a Roses "double" and as they had already won at Headingley the previous Whitsuntide, we had something on our plates. And we all knew it.

In the words of the *Daily Herald* writer, Allan Cave: "In 40 years, I've never seen a county match like it and certainly not a Roses match. Wilson set an amazingly tight field and Trueman (two for 28) and Ryan (five for 50) bowled their hearts out."

In fact it wasn't *quite* like that. Closey suggested we set a defensive field from the start to "make the buggers work for the runs" and that is what we did. Sixteen runs came in the first threequarters of an hour and then the skipper ran out Barber. Duggie Padgett brought off a great running catch in the covers to send back Wharton who had been the chief run-scorer in the first innings. When Ken Grieves came in, Lancashire still needed 50 and amazingly they now had only 55

Brian Close leads off the players at Harrogate after clinching the County Championship in 1967.

minutes to get them. Geoff Pullar had had to struggle for 80 minutes for his 14 runs when I bowled him, and Fred yorked Peter Marner for none: 32-4! Now it was Lancashire who were under pressure but, of course, we still couldn't afford a single mistake.

It gave me immense pleasure to remove Roy Collins' leg stump after which Statham was caught behind: 43-6. Grieves was still giving us problems – sneaking quick singles and messing up our fielding deployment but then came the body-blow: "Chimp" Clayton put up a catch to Vic Wilson off Fred. It was the sort of catch you would expect your wife to take without any problems but Vic, with what were usually the safest pair of hands in the business, put it down! No one wanted to look at anyone else! Grieves finally went for a 27 which had virtually won the game for Lancashire – but we weren't giving up.

The last over arrived with six runs needed. Fred to bowl. I don't think I have ever seen him as charged up even though the two of us had been in action for two hours. The crowd of 10,000 stayed on ... no thought of leaving to catch buses or trains. The tension, the atmosphere, was unbelievable. The crowd, alternately hushed or roaring its collective head off, now subsided into an awed silence. Clayton took a single off the first ball and all Lancashire cheered. Fred bowled Tommy Greenhough with the second and all Yorkshire cheered.

That brought in Jack Dyson who might have hurried to the middle as the circumstances demanded but who was certainly not happy. In fact he looked as though he wished he was dead – or feared he might be any minute now. The ball hit him on the pads. With Clayton backing up furiously and roaring for a single, they set off and I groaned silently as the ball rebounded in my direction. Half-blinded by sweat and almost rigid with tension, I fumbled. And the single became a two. Dyson somehow snatched a single off the fourth ball and Clayton, shuffling forward from the crease, managed one off the fifth. The last ball was now coming up and the scores were tied.

The positioning of the field was a matter of the most elaborate care. The crowd howled for Fred to "get on wi' it" but he waited until every fieldsman was in exactly the position indicated. Then he steamed in ...

Clayton's backing-up had so far been mightily impressive. He now set off almost as Fred was starting his 25-yard run. And when Fred arrived at the stumps he must have been about half-way down the pitch. Fred stopped, looked at Clayton with as much geniality as the situation allowed, and casually remarked, "You've just lost, Sunshine." The ball was in his hand and his hand hovered over the stumps. Clayton's head went down. But Fred did not remove the bails. The age of cricketing chivalry was not yet dead. He tucked the ball into his pocket and marched back to the start of his run.

There was just one more touch of drama to come. Fred, the great competitor, refused to believe any batsman could withstand him when he was utterly determined and he was all of that now. He really ran in and, I think, tried to bowl a leg stump yorker. Dyson afterwards said he was expecting a bouncer and had positioned his feet accordingly.

At the very last minute, Dyson lunged forward, somehow got a faint nick ... and the ball sped away to the fine-leg boundary. Lancashire were home by two wickets.

Now looking at the figures, the time involved, the whole picture, no one could reasonably blame us for not winning. We had made a good effort and it just hadn't worked. But all the odds had been against us since the start of the Lancashire second innings. By any standards we had fought a good fight.

No-one, however, would have thought so on hearing the inquest and the recriminations which started in our dressing-room. The arguments would go on for a long time. Any defeat was a serious matter for Yorkshire in 1960. Defeat in a Roses match was specially hard to bear. But two defeats in one season by Lancashire! That was just a bit *too* much. If Tuesday, 2nd August, 1960, was a cross to bear, I've got to say that it was a day's cricket which will live in my mind forever.

By just after lunch, three days later, we had beaten Notts at Scarborough by an innings and 57 runs. We were back on course. And by the end of the season we had won the championship – again.

YORKSHIRE

First Innings		Second Innings	
W.B. Stott c Marner b Higgs	3	c Collins b Statham	5
K. Taylor b Higgs	24	b Higgs	8
D.E.V. Padgett lbw Greenhough	21	lbw b Statham	6
D.B. Close b Statham	63	lbw b Statham	9
P.J. Sharpe lbw b Statham	16	lbw b Statham	46
R. Illingworth lbw b Statham	7	c Clayton b Dyson	9
J.V. Wilson b Statham	13	c Clayton b Greenhough	20
D. Wilson lbw b Statham	0	not out	32
F.S. Trueman not out	3	lbw b Barber	4
J.G. Binks b Higgs	4	b Higgs	1
M. Ryan b Higgs	0	b Barber	3
Extras	7	Extras	6
Total	154	Total	149

LANCASHIRE

First Innings		Second Innings	
R.W. Barber c Trueman b Wilson D	71	run out	11
G. Pullar c Taylor b Close	11	b Ryan	14
A. Wharton c Wilson JV b Trueman	83	c Padgett b Ryan	4
J. Dyson b Trueman	15	not out	5
K. Grieves lbw b Ryan	5	c Binks b Ryan	27
R. Collins b Trueman	0	b Ryan	2
P. Marner run out	4	b Trueman	15
G. Clayton c Close b Trueman	28	not out	15
T. Greenhough c Sharpe b Ryan	0	b Trueman	0
J.B. Statham c Wilson JV b Ryan	0	c Binks b Ryan	0
K. Higgs not out	3	Did not bat	
Extras	6	Extras	3
Total	226	Total (for 8 wkts)	81

Bowling

YORKSHIRE (first innings): Statham 27-3-43-5; Higgs 17.2-6-48-4; Greenhough 15-2-46-1; J. Dyson 5-2-10-0; Barber 1-1-0-0; (second innings): Statham 24-13-23-4; Higgs 16-7-35-2; Greenhough 16-6-43-1; Dyson 10-6-12-1; Barber 7.3-0-30-0.

LANCASHIRE (first innings): Trueman 28-5-65-4; Ryan 33-9-69-3; Close 12-3-23-1; D. Wilson 13-7-35-1; Illingworth 16-6-28-0; (second innings): Trueman 16-4-28-2; Ryan 15-4-50-5.

8

Mike
Cowan

Warwickshire v Yorkshire
Edgbaston 1960
20th, 22nd, 23rd August

MICHAEL JOSEPH COWAN, *born 10.6.1933, Leeds. Left-arm fast-medium bowler, left-hand bat, who took more wickets (276) than he scored runs (233) in his first-class career. A big-hearted cricketer who might have become one of the outstanding left-arm bowlers but for a back strain sustained while touring Pakistan in 1955-56. He also missed the 1959 season and most of that in 1961 through injury and illness but he always came back – with a smile and a good performance with the ball. Has worked as a representative for Penguin Books since leaving cricket and is an accomplished after-dinner entertainer.*

The county championship season was building up to an exciting climax when we arrived in Birmingham on the evening of Friday, 19th August and what gave it an extra piquance was that our closest rivals were Lancashire, the old enemy. We had lost to them twice that season; it was now absolutely essential that we beat them to the title. It wouldn't quite make up for those two defeats but it would certainly help to make us feel a bit better.

Then things came unstuck at Swansea where we were comprehensively beaten by Glamorgan before lunch on the third day. There was plenty of time for reflection on the way to Birmingham . . .

We were without Freddie Trueman and Duggie Padgett who were playing for England against South Africa at The Oval and we were well pleased to bowl out Warwickshire for a modest 173 on Saturday afternoon and even more pleased when Bryan Stott and Brian Bolus started on a big first-wicket partnership. On the Monday morning they carried on to put 152 runs on the board before Bolus was out. Stottie was in particularly good nick at that time with scores of 75, 18, 33, 1 not out, 52 and 12 in his last six innings. If he had chosen this Warwickshire game as his special memory I wouldn't have been at all surprised because he made 186 out of our first-innings total of 295. So, with a lead of 122, we were in a pretty useful position when Warwickshire went in for the second time with less than an hour to go on the second day.

I must confess to feeling fairly pleased with myself as the third morning began. I had taken three for 44 in the first innings and then grabbed the wickets of Norman Horner and "Billy" Ibadulla before the close of play on Monday. It looked as though my place in the side was going to be secure for the remainder of that season. I should have known better. It wasn't really a good idea to feel secure in the Yorkshire side at that time.

As we went out onto the field at half-past eleven the captain (Vic Wilson) walked beside me and gave me the news that at the end of the match I was to go, with Jackie Birkenshaw (12th man at Edgbaston), to Scarborough to join the second team! It wasn't perhaps the most tactful timing of a message I have ever experienced. It wasn't exactly calculated to fire me up to help bowl out the opposition again.

In fact I felt absolutely gutted and as I took the ball to resume the attack with Mel Ryan all sorts of thoughts were swirling round in my mind – and none of them was about bowling out Warwickshire! It would be totally wrong to say that I didn't try – Pride was too strong for that. But equally it has to be said that I wasn't exactly bowling with a light heart or a fierce determination to remove Jim Stewart and Ray Hitchcock, the overnight batsmen. There were too many other thoughts which kept creeping into my mind to disturb a bowler's concentration. I had not, then, been awarded a Yorkshire Cap; we were not exactly overpaid. I was married, with a young son, and professional cricket was my job. I desperately wanted to make my way as a Yorkshire player but what hope was there? Just when I had been feeling at least reasonably optimistic all my hopes had been dashed . . . second-team cricket the next day!

Stewart and Hitchcock had put on 101 for the third wicket when the second new ball became due and I still, to this day, can't explain what happened next. Call it the glorious uncertainty of cricket if you like. Perhaps it was just that I felt there was no longer any pressure on me to do well. Whatever it was, everything now seemed to click into place. Only those who have played first-class cricket will truly under-stand it all. Suddenly my length was just right; there was just the right degree of in-swing, the occasional movement off the seam . . . everything a left-arm over-the-wicket bowler looks for. Snicks were held (thank you Jimmy Binks and the close-field) and when the batsman missed, I hit – the last three batsmen departed "bowled Cowan".

From a sombre and depressing morning it had become a glorious afternoon. Mel Ryan had bowled Hitchcock early on so there were no distracting thoughts of "all ten" to bother me. I was simply a bowler for whom everything was going well and it felt marvellous. From 130 for two, Warwickshire slumped to 162 all out, I had taken nine for 43 and the new-ball spell had yielded me seven for 11. How good it felt! We were left to make 41 to win and it was all over before tea.

As I was applauded from the field, the first recognisable face in the crowd that I saw was that of the landlord of my local pub, in Doncaster. His news was that Lancashire had not got the result *they* wanted: we were top of the table. And Vic Wilson came over in the dressing-room and said I had "better remain with the first team" which was now going on to play Somerset.

I don't know whether he had taken that decision himself or whether it resulted from a quick 'phone call to Leeds but I do know that

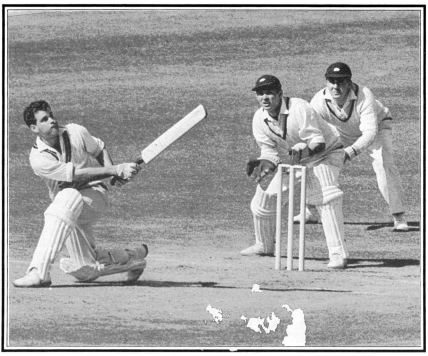

*Jimmy Binks and Philip Sharpe look on as Ted Clark sweeps Don Wilson for three in
the match against Middlesex at Lord's in 1962. (Photo by S&G Press Agency)*

the party for the three remaining games had been selected a week
previously, *irrespective of possible performances.*

Now I stayed in the side as we drew with Somerset in a rain-ruined
game, beat Worcs at Harrogate and then drew the return match at
Worcester. The results were enough to give us the county championship and I finished the season with championship figures of 701.4
overs, 174 maiden, 1505 runs, 66 wickets at 22.81. I was still not
capped; the future was still uncertain.

At the Scarborough Festival where the county champions (as in the
previous year) were given a memorable ovation, I asked for a personal
interview with Brian Sellers, our formidable chairman.

I explained to him that I was married, with a young son. I badly
wanted to remain a Yorkshire player but other counties had "sounded
me out" and if Yorkshire did not need me, could I be released? If
Yorkshire decided that I *was* required, then could my pay be increased?
As things were, I simply could not manage.

All this was delivered while facing the famous Sellers glare. Players
of other counties used to complain about the difficulties of batting
while Brian Close's furrowed brow, frowning in concentration, hovered
a yard or two from them. All I can say is that they were lucky not to
have had to contend with the Sellers glare when they were *off* the field.

However, on this occasion he heard me out and I shall never forget his response: "Fair enough. I promise you more money."

Startled, but vastly relieved, I stammered my thanks and turned to go. The Crackerjack then added, "Thanks for coming to see me. I appreciate it. I get sick of asking some of the others if they've wiped their arses in the morning."

The season finished, I took my wife, Judy, and the ten-month-old Shaun on holiday to Newquay. It was closed! One morning, reading the *Daily Telegraph* in a cafe, I saw the headline: "Yorkshire award 4 Caps" and the names printed below were Sharpe, Bolus, Don Wilson and Cowan.

Perhaps my final memory of Edgbaston, 1960, is provided by the words of spectator Len Hutton (long before Jimmy Greaves had seized on the phrase): "It's a funny old game." No one who has played will argue with that.

WARWICKSHIRE

First Innings		Second Innings	
N.F. Horner c Illingworth b Close	11	lbw b Cowan	19
K. Ibadulla b Close	21	c Wilson JV b Cowan	5
W.J. Stewart b Taylor	20	c Close b Cowan	60
R.E. Hitchcock c Binks b Ryan	3	b Ryan	42
T.W. Cartwright b Ryan	3	lbw b Cowan	0
D.L. Amiss c and b Ryan	30	c Wilson JV b Cowan	3
A.C. Smith c Binks b Cowan	51	not out	22
J.D. Bannister c Wilson D b Cowan	17	c Binks b Cowan	1
A. Wright c Binks b Ryan	4	b Cowan	0
R.G. Carter lbw b Cowan	2	b Cowan	2
O.S. Wheatley not out	2	b Cowan	0
Extras	7	Extras	8
Total	173	Total	162

YORKSHIRE

First Innings		Second Innings	
W.B. Stott c Wheatley b Carter	186	c Cartwright b A.C. Smith	10
J.B. Bolus c A.C. Smith b Cartwright	56	not out	15
P.J. Sharpe lbw b Cartwright	1	not out	14
D.B. Close run out	14		
K. Taylor c A.C. Smith b Bannister	0		
R. Illingworth c A.C. Smith b Wheatley	2		
J.V. Wilson c A.C. Smith b Bannister	5		
D. Wilson c Horner b Wheatley	1		
J.G. Binks b Amiss	21		
M. Ryan b Carter	3		
M.J. Cowan not out	0		
Extras	6	Extras	2
Total	295	Total (for 1 wicket)	41

Bowling
WARWICKSHIRE (first innings): Ryan 21-5-44-4; Cowan 20.1-4-44-3; Close 19-6-27-2; Taylor 10-3-26-1; Illingworth 15-11-13-0; D. Wilson 3-1-12-0; (second innings): Ryan 26-9-48-1; Cowan 27.2-11-43-9; Close 6-3-13-0; Taylor 14-3-33-0; Illingworth 15-11-9-0; D. Wilson 10-8-8-0.
YORKSHIRE (first innings): Bannister 25-8-46-2; Wheatley 29-7-66-2; Wright 22-3-66-0; Cartwright 21-6-58-2; Carter 14.1-6-23-2; Amiss 9-2-26-1; Hitchcock 1-0-4-0; (second innings): Bannister 3-0-10-0; Wheatley 3-0-6-0; A.C. Smith 3.5-0-5-1; Ibadulla 2-0-13-0; Horner 1-0-5-0.

9

Don
Wilson

Worcestershire v Yorkshire
Worcester 1961
3rd, 5th, 6th June

DONALD WILSON, *born 7.8.1937, Settle. Slow left-arm bowler, vigorous left-hand batsman, good fielder. Played 392 matches for Yorkshire between 1957 and 1974, taking well over 1,000 wickets, scoring nearly 6,000 runs and holding 250 catches. Played in six Tests and toured Australia, New Zealand and India/Ceylon. After retiring he coached in South Africa before becoming chief coach at the MCC School at Lord's. Now Director of Sport and Sport Development at Ampleforth College.*

It must surely be every bowler's dream to play at least one memorable innings in his life – an innings which changes the course of the game, perhaps even one which *wins* the game.

My chance came at Worcester on Tuesday, 6th June, 1961. It is perhaps as well I made the most of it because I didn't play again for Yorkshire that season! It was a reasonable game in many ways. How often do you see one side total exactly the same figures in both first and second innings? But that's more a matter for the statisticians. My involvement was more personal.

In the Worcs first innings I had taken a knock on the thumb of my left hand. Off I went to hospital where a hair-line fracture was diagnosed and I was put in plaster from elbow to fingers. Still, I didn't feel much like being left out of things altogether and when Yorkshire reached 295 for nine, giving a lead of 38, I was padded up and heading out to bat at No.11 when the captain signalled that he had declared. And now I couldn't bowl, either!

It was a special kind of torture to have to sit and watch it all happen, especially when we got into trouble almost from the start of the second innings. Our target was 189 but we lost the first four wickets cheaply; then Illingworth and the captain (Vic Wilson) had a partnership which put us back on course. Three more wickets then fell and it was now Jimmy Banks who came to the rescue with an innings of 46, described by one newspaper as "probably the most significant of his life". When *he* was out it was 154 for nine and this time nobody was going to stop me getting involved. The captain was strongly against it but I managed to win that argument and went out to join that well-known batsman R.K. Platt (of whom you will find more, elsewhere in this book) who also bowled a bit. It was our duty to save the game.

Plattie had been showing his mettle for half-an-hour when I joined him and he'll tell you that while *he* was perfectly content, he wasn't too sure about his one-handed partner. It wasn't too bad at the start. Flavell and Coldwell had done the early damage and they were a pair everyone respected. In fact, Jack Flavell took 171 wickets in that 1961 season and was picked by England in four Tests; Coldwell was capped the following year.

But when they had a rest, the spinners took over – Norman Gifford (left-arm) and Martin Horton (off-breaks). They cleared out the middle order but they didn't bowl particularly well at us. In fact, Norman allowed me the luxury of a one-handed sweep for four and I was beginning to enjoy myself. Saving the game didn't seem all that difficult.

Then, with a 5.30pm finish looming and five minutes or so to play in the last half-hour, George Dews (skippering Worcs in that game) decided to take the new ball. This *wasn't* so good. Thoughts flickered through my mind like "it's not cricket" and phrases like "playing the game" came readily to mind. Would Jim Swanton have approved of it? What would the members have said at Lord's? The new ball against Numbers ten and eleven, one with a broken thumb and his arm in plaster?

But the new ball was in Flavell's hands and he must have fancied his chances a bit. The last pair in front of him, needing 23 to win in, now, just under five minutes and one of the batsmen, the one now facing him, could only grip the bat properly with one hand! Oh yes, he must have fancied his chances. I could see the shine on the gleaming new ball as he ran in. I hit him straight for four. He said something very rude. I pushed into the covers for two and he said something even ruder. Would you believe it – he next bowled a bouncer! Now if it had been delivered straight at the throat I would have had a bit of bother with it. But it wasn't straight. It gave me a bit of room and I hit it over the covers for four.

Mr Flavell was not amused. His next remark included the phrase "spawny bastard" but was embellished with other adjectives I can't mention here. In the meantime my partner had come down the pitch to hiss at me, "For God's sale, Wils. We're supposed to be trying to save this game, not win it." Mr Flavell overheard this and it didn't improve his temper much. He bowled one which I missed – and so did the wicket-keeper; four byes. I don't remember the next but I hit the last one, an on-drive, for four. We needed five to win off the last over. Would you believe it? – Plattie blocked the first ball! It was now my turn to address a few remarks to my partner. He pushed a single. We reached the fourth ball of Coldwell's over and I decided not to leave any more to chance. I advanced down the pitch and hit him back over his head for a lofted four. Well, most of the fieldsmen were crowded round the bat, weren't they? And we'd won. My dream had come true.

Plattie, so recently the apprehensive pessimist, gawped for a minute – then danced a jig in the middle of the pitch. I joined him. The Worcs bowlers and fielders slunk away wondering how they were going to explain this to other teams around the circuit.

"Cricket's most courageous story of the summer," was how Alex Bannister described it in the *Daily Mail*. "Incredible," was J.M. Kilburn's verdict in *The Yorkshire Post*. I must say that Jim was not always my most ardent admirer but he did me proud on this occasion. "Figures mark the facts," he went on, "but this was fancy beyond the fanciful and it began, 'Once upon a time . . .'." Well, I think that may be taken as a compliment, don't you?

My batting peers came in for a bit of stick in that second innings, in fact: "Trueman hit one six and was caught at long-on seeking a second." And the one I really liked: "Close was caught at cover from a back-foot stroke of greater originality than wisdom." Nice, that, isn't it? Good old Closey.

Well, if the story began "Once upon a time . . ." it really ought to end ". . . and they all lived happily ever after." Alas, I can't say that. I didn't play for Yorkshire again in 1961. But I did a lot of dreaming.

And if Bob Platt ever tries to tell you about his batting (which I am sure he will) just say to him, "Worcester, 1961." That'll shut him up if nothing else will.

WORCESTERSHIRE

First Innings		Second Innings	
D. Kenyon c Wilson b Trueman	30	c Wilson V b Bainbridge	34
M.J. Horton b Platt	13	c Binks b Trueman	6
R.G.A. Headley st Binks b Close	61	c Binks b Trueman	49
D.W. Richardson c Close			
b Illingworth	23	c sub b Close	5
G. Dews c Stott b Illingworth	47	b Bainbridge	14
R.G. Broadbent b Illingworth	5	b Trueman	4
R. Booth lbw b Illingworth	6	run out	31
J.A. Standen b Close	0	b Bainbridge	23
N. Gifford not out	6	not out	12
L.J. Coldwell c and b Close	4	b Trueman	25
J.A. Flavell c Wilson V b Close	2	c Padgett b Platt	11
Extras	30	Extras	13
Total	227	Total	227

YORKSHIRE

First Innings		Second Innings	
W.B. Stott c Dews b Horton	46	c Standen b Flavell	5
J.B. Bolus c Standen b Gifford	54	b Coldwell	5
D.E.V. Padgett c Booth b Horton	6	c sub b Flavell	7
D.B. Close c sub b Horton	11	c sub b Flavell	15
R. Illingworth c Headley b Horton	5	lbw b Coldwell	42
J.V. Wilson run out	49	lbw b Horton	16
F.S. Trueman b Coldwell	43	c Flavell b Gifford	7
A.B. Bainbridge c Standen b Horton	24	b Horton	0
J.G. Binks c Richardson b Flavell	19	b Flavell	46
R.K. Platt not out	0	not out	7
D. Wilson did not bat		not out	29
Extras	8	Extras	12
Total (for 9 wkts dec)	265	Total (for 9 wkts)	191

Bowling

WORCESTERSHIRE (first innings): Trueman 14-4-33-1; Platt 15-5-43-1; Illingworth 29-13-47-4; Wilson 2-1-13-0; Bainbridge 18-8-34-0; Close 9.1-3-27-4; (second innings): Trueman 27-9-56-4; Platt 17.3-6-43-1; Close 14-4-69-1; Bainbridge 31-16-52-3.

YORKSHIRE (first innings): Flavell 16-4-38-1; Coldwell 10-4-22-1; Gifford 40-18-74-1; Horton 44-18-110-5; Standen 5-1-13-1; (second innings): Flavell 24-10-44-5; Coldwell 10.4-7-17-2; Gifford 34-15-80-1; Horton 19-7-37-2.

10

Keith Gillhouley

Yorkshire v Essex
Harrogate 1961
7th, 8th, 9th June

K EITH GILLHOULEY, *born 8.8.1934, Huddersfield. Right-hand batsman, slow left-arm bowler. Although he played for Yorkshire in only one year, Keith Gillhouley had a remarkable 1961 season. Called up after Don Wilson had been injured at Worcester in June, he completed the season as Yorkshire's slow left-armer and took 73 wickets, behind Trueman and Illingworth. He also scored 306 runs. With no place for him the following season he joined Notts where he settled and established his own business.*

Nothing in my cricketing memories will ever equal the experience of playing for Yorkshire for the first time. It was like a dream come true, and I was no starry-eyed youngster at the time; I was 26 years old.

But most of those 26 years had been spent listening to my father telling me of the cricketing giants who had played for Yorkshire... their records, their personal characteristics. I do believe my father genuinely thought that Wilfred Rhodes had been directly descended from The Almighty and when he had a son who bowled slow left-arm... well, all things became possible, I suppose.

Personally, I thought my time might have come and gone. I was an all-rounder pro for Dalton in the Huddersfield League, batting at No.4, and had taken 91 wickets at 14.25 for Yorkshire Colts in 1960. But Don Wilson had the first-team spot and had been awarded his senior cap in the same year as I got my Second XI cap. What a day that had been! Chris Balderstone, John Hampshire and I had been told that we had been "capped" during a Second XI game at Sunderland and we telephoned through to Leeds to ask Bill Sutcliffe if he would keep his shop open late so we could collect our caps, ties and sweaters.

Bless him, Bill did just that and after we had collected our gear he said, "Well, you are now all going to have a pint on me." So it was quite late when I got home but my wife, Mitzi, said, "Let's go and see your father." I honestly thought that my career could go no higher than that.

Anyway, in June, 1961, I was playing in a second team game at Ripon. I was sitting at tea, wondering how I had been bowled round my legs when Ted Lester, the captain, told me I was wanted by the first team to play against Essex at Harrogate the following day. I simply couldn't believe it and I couldn't wait to get home to tell Mitzi, who had always been very supportive. And again she said, "I can't wait to see your father's face when you tell him." So off we went – on two buses because we had no car – and Dad said, very quietly, "Oh, good." It wasn't, perhaps *quite* the reaction I might have expected but I saw the blood drain from his face and the eyes open very wide. He was, quite simply, lost for words. I think he was overawed by the thought that he might have bred a new Wardle, or a Verity, or even... but no. There couldn't ever be another Rhodes. But just at that moment it was enough that I would be playing for Yorkshire at Harrogate the following day.

For ten minutes or so Dad was away in a world of his own, dreaming his dreams. Then he recovered sufficiently to say, "Let's go down to the Griffin." In the pub I sensed that he was dying to tell everyone the news but he daren't let my mother hear him say a word which might embarrass me. For my part, I wanted to shout the news, too, but that just wasn't the done thing. But finally Dad said he would just have a walk round the bowling green "to see who was there" and soon the news was all round the place.

It now seemed that everyone who had bowled at me at school had, in fact, bowled me out; everyone had hit me into the Forresters' car park when we played with a tennis ball down "Poky Nick". That seemed to apply to all the adults, years older than me, those coming into the pub and, more particularly, those leaving it. But they all wished me well – and reminded me of their part in my development! The following day (after my first day in first-class cricket) everyone in the Griffin knew what had happened at Harrogate – but they all wanted the details as well, even the bus conductor.

But what of that first day's play? Well, most of the team were known to me from Second XI or schools cricket and Federation games, except Brian Close and Jimmy Binks. Close was captain in the absence of Vic Wilson and his reputation, in the Huddersfield district at any rate, was of being a "big head". How wrong that proved to be! He did everything right as my first captain in county cricket. He was considerate and he boosted my confidence; his instructions were simple and straightforward; his field-placing was immaculate and I don't think his tactics could have been bettered. He was helpful in that game and all the others in which I played that season. Even when I moved to Notts he was *still* helpful and whenever I could, I sought him out, and Ray Illingworth, so I could learn something. Closey actually told me how I could get him out or at least prevent him "lapping" (sweeping) me and he wasn't kidding.

I travelled to Harrogate with Mel Ryan. We arrived in plenty of time; the sun was shining, the covers off and the groundsman putting the finishing touches to his pitch. I looked around at some of the figures I had only read about, like Trevor Bailey, particularly sun-tanned; not as tall as I had thought him to be but full of character. I remembered how he and Willie Watson had seen off the Australians, Lindwall, Miller and Johnston, eight years earlier.

I had a cup of tea in the dressing-room but I needed to be "doing

Yorkshire players celebrate winning the County Championship in 1967. Shown are (left to right): Philip Sharpe, Richard Hutton, Don Wilson, Brian Close, George Alcock (physio), Fred Trueman, Tony Nicholson. Front: Ray Illingworth, Geoff Boycott. (Photo by Jack Hickes)

something". I had always enjoyed cricket at Harrogate with the Second team and with the Federation side and I remembered how a girl had sent in a bag of toffees after I had made 68 with the Federation. The crowd seemed a lot bigger now and with that particular interest in new faces to the first team – myself and Brian Bainbridge, the off-spinner from Middlesbrough. One could sense a certain inquisitiveness but one feeling was very clear, that the whole of Yorkshire was behind us, willing us to do well.

Back in the dressing-room, telegrams were arriving – from friends and team-mates in the Colts, from the President of the Huddersfield League, from former club colleagues who had helped me in many ways along the way, with coaching, advice and a bit of discipline when it was needed. I was being carried along by a wave of support.

We won the toss and batted but the sky had clouded over and it wasn't easy. Bailey, from close to the stumps, was moving the ball both ways and we didn't total 200. I was out for one, hitting across the line. Not much glory there! When we took the field, I was fielding at gulley in a position that seemed uncomfortably close for me. I didn't see myself as emulating Sellers and Mitchell in close-to-the-bat positions as my father had described them fielding! But I didn't have to wait too long before the captain gave me the ball and asked me what field I wanted. I was in something of a daze and I couldn't answer but Closey didn't make any comment and put the field in position. I marked out my run and noticed that the crowd seemed to be very close to the field of play. It was a daunting and wonderful moment.

I was saying to myself, "Line and length. Nowt short. You can't have fielders everywhere so bowl to your field. And don't bowl down t'leg side." – all the basics I had had drilled into me from the age of 14 by coaches, captains – and by opposing batsmen!

I remembered that Arnold Hamer (later with Derbyshire) and a 17-year-old Ken Taylor (now a team-mate) had given me some almighty tap when playing for Primrose Hill in the Huddersfield League and I recalled the mid-wicket fieldsmen ducking as the ball rebounded from the wall of the Crimea pub. And it's no use bowling wide of the off stump so there is no tap: you've got to make the batsman *play* at the ball.

My first over at Harrogate might have been a maiden; in any case, the crowd gave it a good reception and that warmed me. Having once ranged the bowling, it then becomes easy to bowl accurately, all other things being equal. I had cultivated concentration which you need to bowl long spells and Ted Lester had been a great help when he was skippering the Colts. And it needs a good captain to pull the strings, so to speak. I had one.

A bit later, Jo Milner, the South African, was driving me hard on the off side and Closey said, "Do you want him to hit you there or do you want him to try to hit against the spin, on the on-side?" I thought to myself, "This must be the sort of conversation Wilfred Rhodes had with his captain but it's a bit much for me." I don't think I replied. Anyway, Closey moved himself from short extra cover to short gulley, positively *inviting* Milner to drive into the covers. It was the first time – but most assuredly not the last – that I found the captain actually *engineering* a situation which invited a batsman to bring about his own destruction. The very next ball was lofted to extra cover ... and the catch dropped! But it illustrated quite clearly to me the extra dimension of Close's conception of cricket, particularly in the field.

As for my concentration, it might well be called, in modern terminology, *self-hypnosis* but no one in the side interfered with this, no one distracted me. I was to find later, in other sides, that there was a bit more frivolity in the field and players didn't like it when I asked them not to engage me in conversation when I was bowling. No one had to be told that in the Yorkshire team of the 1960s.

It was nice to get that first wicket but the reaction of the team was even more gratifying. The congratulations were led by Bryan Stott who, from my first glimpse of him playing for Airedale and Wharfedale boys against Huddersfield boys, seemed to place great value on doing things the right way. And as the new batsman came to the wicket there was just time for Bryan to give me a quick lesson on how to keep the ball shiny by rubbing any bruising of the cover with spit until it was dull and tacky, then polishing up *on the sock* to get back the shine.

That kept the flannels immaculate. I can't imagine Fred using that method but, thinking about it later, I realised Stottie was always concerned to keep *his* immaculate appearance. If I mention this in jocular style, it doesn't mean that I hadn't taken the hint: Bryan was stressing the importance of team-play and thinking of the seamers who had to come back later. For my part, I needed one side of the ball shiny because I liked to mix in an occasional in-swinger. Jimmy Binks used to tell me he could see it coming a mile off but it still surprised a few batsmen. And I managed to surprise Jimmy once, too.

Playing against him at Trent Bridge, I'd had a long spell and got some tidy figures on a good pitch. Jimmy came in for a late slog – and I decided to bowl him a swinger from round the wicket. As my arm came over I saw his face break into a huge smile – he was telling me he had "picked" it – and the ball pitched exactly right. Jimmy missed it by a foot and we both started laughing. But he had the last word: slogged me for a quick 20-odd and spoiled my figures.

But back to Harrogate, I can't remember much about the wickets except for the dismissal of Gordon Barker late on the second day. He pushed forward and as the ball dropped from somewhere about the splice, Closey (positioned in one of his lunatic positions at short gulley) threw himself quite literally under the bat to catch the ball! Gordon departed shaking his head; Brian rose to his feet with that grim smile of huge satisfaction which was so well-known on the cricket fields of England.

As we struggled a bit on a slow turner in the second innings, Closey was again a great help: "Play for your wicket against the off-spinner and if it's pitched up, hit it." I did and got a few runs which, I suppose, helped towards our win and, ultimately, another championship. If I had never played again, I would have been happy.

I felt I hadn't let anyone down, through that whole range of people who wished we well, and my hometown. Just as importantly, I had repaid in some small way the debt I owed to Mitzi, to my parents and all those people who had helped with instruction, encouragement and advice. I had played for Yorkshire.

Now I know something of what Welsh rugby players feel when they are selected for their country. Even today I understand and identify with the emotion they experience when I see them line up before the kick-off at Cardiff Arms Park. It is, quite simply, what *I* felt in playing cricket for Yorkshire.

YORKSHIRE

First Innings		Second Innings	
W.B. Stott lbw b Bailey	14	lbw b Bailey	4
J.B. Bolus lbw b Preston	11	lbw b Bailey	3
D.E.V. Padgett c Taylor b Bailey	0	c Barker b Bailey	7
D.B. Close c Taylor b Preston	24	b Phelan	71
K. Taylor b Hobbs	9	b Phelan	22
P.J. Sharpe c Taylor b Greensmith	82	c Milner b Phelan	0
K. Gillhouley lbw b Preston	1	lbw b Bailey	16
J.G. Binks c Taylor b Hobbs	5	b Preston	34
A.B. Bainbridge lbw b Greensmith	18	c Milner b Phelan	0
M. Ryan not out	9	not out	17
R.K. Platt c Preston b Hobbs	0	b Phelan	5
Extras	2	Extras	2
Total	175	Total	181

ESSEX

First Innings		Second Innings	
G.E. Barker b Binks b Bainbridge	16	c Close b Gillhouley	13
G.J. Smith lbw b Gillhouley	16	c Close b Platt	56
B. Taylor b Bainbridge	5	b Bainbridge	8
J. Milner st Binks b Gillhouley	15	c Close b Bainbridge	0
T.E. Bailey lbw b Bainbridge	1	b Bainbridge	10
L.A. Savill c Sharpe b Gillhouley	15	c Binks b Bainbridge	22
M. Bear lbw b Gillhouley	0	b Platt	20
W.T. Greensmith not out	6	c and b Bainbridge	20
P.J. Phelan c Sharpe b Bainbridge	0	b Platt	11
R. Hobbs c Close b Bainbridge	0	not out	8
K.C. Preston c Binks b Bainbridge	29	c Close b Bainbridge	2
Extras	3	Extras	11
Total	123	Total	181

Bowling
YORKSHIRE (first innings): Bailey 21-5-35-2; Preston 21-3-59-3; Phelan 7-2-14-0; Hobbs 13.4-3-31-3; Greensmith 7-0-34-2; (second innings): Bailey 26-7-54-4; Preston 14-1-23-1; Phelan 16.4-2-74-5; Hobbs 5-1-28-0.
ESSEX (first innings): Gillhouley 27-15-35-4; Bainbridge 23.4-5-58-6; M. Ryan 3-0-14-0; Platt 7-3-13-0; (second innings): Close 8-2-20-0; Taylor 1-0-1-0; Gillhouley 18-4-47-1; Bainbridge 27-10-53-6; Ryan 2-0-5-0; Platt 15.2-3-44-3.

11

Duggie Padgett

Yorkshire v MCC
Scarborough 1961
9th, 11th, 12th September

DOUGLAS ERNEST VERNON PADGETT, *born 20.7.1934, Idle (Bradford). Right-hand batsman. One of the most graceful and technically-correct batsmen to play for the county, he scored 21,124 runs and held 261 catches. He hit 1,000 runs on a season on 12 occasions and in 1959 reached 2,181 at an average of 41.15. Played twice for England the following season. He has retained his connection with the club and is the senior county coach at Headingley.*

Readers may have noticed that in the biographical notes to this chapter there is no mention whatsoever of my bowling. Nowhere in Yorkshire's records of "exceptional pieces of bowling" does my name figure. Even though I retired after 1971 with 21 years service I had to wait another 13 years to receive the grudging credit (in the 1984 Cricketers Who's Who): "Right-arm medium pace bowler".

This has to be seen not only as less than gracious but less than adequate. "Medium pace" covers a great deal of mediocrity. In all truth, and with complete modesty, I could claim to bowl *the lot* as my record plainly shows. The strike-rate was exceptional, the economy-rate impressive (at times remarkable) and my list of victims would look pretty good in any company.

The fact of the matter is that I found it very difficult throughout my career to get on to bowl. In the early days there were people like Trueman, Appleyard, Wardle, Illingworth and Close ahead of me in the queue and it had to be said that none of them was too keen on anyone else nipping in to steal their thunder. In later years Trueman was still with us; so were Close and Illingworth and at various times there were a dozen or more others who were given the ball by a number of captains far more often than I got it. They, of course, were non-batsmen and so their reputations stood or fell by what they achieved with the ball. Some, like Platt, have made extravagant – even outrageous – claims which need not be taken seriously but they were all given precedence over me when it came to bowling. Only when the situation was otherwise hopeless and all the recognised bowlers had failed did a captain toss the ball to Padgett. Who can tell what our record might have been like in the ten years from 1959 onwards if I had been given the recognition I deserved? If ever there was a bowler for all seasons and all situations it was DEV Padgett. But let the record speak for itself:

1959: Scarborough, in September. The county matches were over, the championship won and MCC were piling up a massive score against Yorkshire in the first match of the Festival. Peter Sainsbury and Roy Booth were engaged in a seventh-wicket partnership which

*Yorkshire players lift the Gillette Cup in 1969 at Lord's after beating Derbyshire.
(Photo by S&G Press Agency)*

had already passed the 100 mark. Trueman, Close, Wilson, Illingworth, Birkenshaw and even Bolus had done their utmost and still the total mounted. I chafed and fretted in the outfield but I knew that moment had to come... On the second morning, MCC still batting, Ronnie Burnet finally called me up.

Now I wasn't exactly what you might call loose, or limbered up, so I concentrated on line and length while I probed for the weakness. Then... with startling pace off the pitch I got right through Booth's defence and bowled him quite comprehensively: 5-1-13-1.

Incredibly, the new captain, Vic Wilson, did not call upon me to bowl throughout the entire 1960 season.

1961: Scarborough again, the MCC match again and it was, in fact, the 75th anniversary of the Festival. The Duke of Edinburgh flew down from Balmoral to watch the first day's play but missed the drama of the third day. Edrich and Dexter in full cry... MCC chasing 203 to win in two hours... and Vic Wilson at last remembered what had happened two years before. He gave me the ball and I lured John Edrich forward, tempting him to drive. He failed to notice I had held the ball back just a bit, mistimed his shot and I threw up the return catch in triumph. Edrich, scorer of nearly 40,000 runs in his career, one of the great Test openers of the post-war era... down he went: 5-1-14-1.

1962: Taunton. Fred Rumsey had been ill-advised enough to bowl a playful bouncer at Fred Trueman when Fred was having a bit of fun thumping the ball about in the Yorkshire second innings. Rumsey claimed later that he had been *told* to do it by his captain, Harold Stephenson, but FST clearly wasn't interested in what the explanation was; his feathers were ruffled. There was only time for a couple of overs before the close but Stephenson sent out Rumsey and Brian Langford (numbers 9 and 11 in the order) to open the innings. Trueman, with murder in his eyes and blood-curdling threats on his lips, marked out a run damn near to the boundary-line and was all ready to bowl the biggest, fastest bouncer of all time when he found Closey had given the new ball to John Hampshire. All Fred's pleas and threats failed to move the captain who apparently didn't want blood and teeth all over the place. He gave the second over to me. It was nice to have that shiny new ball in my hands for a change. I gave Rumsey a four to lull him into a false sense of security, then pushed one through. It knocked his off hob back many a mile: 0.5-0-4-1.

1964: Bramall Lane, Sheffield, and this time my victim, another opening batsman, was called Harvey – not, unfortunately the Australian Harvey, though I'd have been glad to have a go at him, but John Frank Harvey, of Derbyshire, a handy sort of lad who played over 200 first-class games. I moved the ball off the seam, forced him into error, found the edge and FS Trueman took the catch.

1965: v Gloucs at Lydney. We didn't often play out in the Forest of Dean and the pitch proved a bit lively, so much so that we bowled out Gloucs for 87 and got 160 in reply. Closey must have been having one of those aberrations of his in the second innings because everybody had a bowl except him... even Jimmy Binks, the wicket-keeper. Gloucs ended up at 80 for two... and who got the wickets? Trueman and Padgett. I bowled Sid Russell with a trimmer... pitched about middle and took the top off the off-stump. I was sorry about it later because Sid was sacked at the end of that season but it was another top-order batsman in my bag: 6-4-6-1.

1967: Derbyshire again and the last first-class victim of my career was Michael Harry Page, a No.3 batsman, who was nearly called up by Yorkshire because he had lived for most of his life in Hull but at the last minute he was found to have been born in Blackpool. I drew him forward, beat him completely in the air and he gave me a return catch: 8-6-6-1. This so utterly demoralised Pagey that he gave up cricket and has spent most of the rest of his life playing golf.

Now I hope those examples start people searching for an answer to the question: why didn't Padgett get more chances to bowl? It was something I could never understand and I can't help feeling that with a little more consideration from my captains we might have been celebrating ten championships between 1959 and 1968, not just seven. Now I have the problem of deciding which of those victims was the most important, which of the games most significant... it'll have to be Edrich, and the MCC match at Scarborough. I rate all the batsmen I dismissed very highly and all the wickets gave me great satisfaction. But, on balance, perhaps John Edrich just has the edge on the others. His record was good and at the time he was in full cry. His dismissal put the brake on the scoring and ruined any possibility of a defeat for Yorkshire.

YORKSHIRE

First Innings		Second Innings	
W.B. Stott c Atkinson b D. Smith	0	c Ingleby-Mackenzie b Knight	21
J.B. Bolus lbw b Bailey	54	lbw b D. Smith	29
D.E.V. Padgett b Knight	12	lbw b Bailey	15
D.B. Close c M. Smith b Bailey	20	b Bailey	13
P.J. Sharpe c Atkinson b Dexter	8	lbw b Bailey	1
R. Illingworth c Parks b Knight	41	lbw b D. Smith	34
J.V. Wilson b Bailey	76	not out	79
F.S. Trueman b D. Allen	5	b D. Allen	5
J.G. Binks c Parks b D. Smith	21	c Parks b Dexter	30
R.K. Platt run out	8	c Parks b Bailey	6
M. Ryan not out	1	not out	7
Extras	14	Extras	9
Total	260	Total (for 9 wkts dec)	249

MCC

First Innings		Second Innings	
J.H. Edrich c Binks b Ryan	58	c and b Padgett	41
G. Atkinson c Bolus b Ryan	49	b Ryan	6
E.R. Dexter not out	118	b Ryan	24
M.J.K. Smith c Wilson b Bolus	68	not out	24
J.M. Parks c Binks b Bolus	2	not out	8
A.C.D. Ingleby-Mackenzie c Sharpe b Trueman	8		
Extras	4	Extras	5
Total (for 5 wkts dec)	307	Total (for 3 wkts)	108

Bowling
YORKSHIRE (first innings): D. Smith 21-1-57-2; Knight 16-4-54-2; Bailey 15.1-1-43-3; Dexter 14-2-39-1; D. Allen 9-3-38-1; M. Allen 5-0-25-0; (second innings): D. Smith 19-0-61-2; Knight 9-1-44-1; Bailey 21-4-38-4; D. Allen 19-7-47-1; M. Allen 3-0-25-0; Dexter 8-1-25-1.
MCC (first innings): Trueman 22-3-67-1; Platt 17-3-76-0; Ryan 24-3-79-2; Close 6-0-22-0; Illingworth 18-4-43-0; Bolus 3-0-16-2. (second innings): Trueman 8-2-38-0; Ryan 7-0-26-2; Illingworth 1-0-4-0; Bolus 5-1-21-0; Padgett 5-1-14-1.

12

Vic Wilson

Yorkshire v Glamorgan
Harrogate 1962
5th, 6th, 7th September

JOHN VICTOR WILSON, *born 17.1.1921, Scampston. Left-hand batsman, fine close fieldsman. Played 477 matches for Yorkshire between 1946-62, scoring 21,650 runs and holding 548 catches. Toured Australia and New Zealand with MCC in 1954-55. Captained Yorkshire 1960-61-62 when the team won the County Championship twice and were runners-up in the middle year. Also played soccer for Leeds United. Farms near Malton.*

The St. George's Road ground at Harrogate had a reasonable record in the 1960s of staging matches which decided the championship. It started in my first year as captain, 1960, when we saw off Worcs by nine wickets.

The cricket always seemed to be good and eventful. In that 1960 game, for instance, F.S. Trueman enlivened the proceedings by hitting 50 in about half-an-hour with five sixes and three fours, and while we didn't always have good weather, the cricket was invariably interesting.

It was especially important to me that we should beat Glamorgan in 1962. I was retiring after 17 seasons and as I had been the captain for three years I was naturally anxious, if possible, to go out on a high note. We *had* to beat Glamorgan to take the title. There was, in consequence, tremendous interest in the game and I believe well over 27,000 people watched it – in spite of the rain.

It was damp when I won the toss and asked Glamorgan to bat first. We hadn't been going very long when Fred (Trueman) decided there was something wrong with the length of the pitch and asked me to have it re-measured. Well, that was a new one, at least! The groundsman produced his chain and the length of the pitch was established as correct to the umpires' satisfaction, if not to Fred's.

But as the pitch began to dry it was Don Wilson who took a liking to it. He returned six for 24 which were his best figures up to that point, although he had several better in the following years. Twice, I remember, he had to dive full length and stretch out those long arms of his to take catches off his own bowling to dismiss Jim Pressdee and Don Shepherd. Glamorgan were all out for 65.

We didn't fare all that much better. Shepherd bowled his off-breaks at round about medium pace and Ossie Wheatley cut down *his* pace to get maximum response from the pitch. It was an innings of 67 by Ken Taylor which helped us to a first-innings lead of 36. By the end of the first day both sides had completed the first innings and Glamorgan were in again, 13 for no wicket.

There seemed to be thousands in the ground on the second morning, no doubt anticipating something just as eventful but when it wasn't raining hard it was drizzling. How patient cricket spectators can be at

Surrey's John Edrich is caught by Jimmy Binks, bowled by Bob Platt, at the Oval in 1959. (Photo by Central Press)

times! By tea-time, half the ground was under water and it seemed impossible that we would be able to play on the final day.

But one should never under-estimate the enthusiasm and ingenuity of cricket people. The spectators living near the ground – and St. George's Road is in the middle of a pleasant suburb – went home and returned with gardening forks! The Harrogate ground staff is not a large one by any means but the head groundsman, Bert Wilson, now found he had scores of volunteer helpers. They were on parade again at 5am on the last morning. More were available if needed because the ground was filled to bursting-point at 11am. By a miracle, the game could resume on time! Now we had to bowl out Glamorgan as quickly as possible and score whatever runs were going to be required.

We were doing quite well until Don Ward and David Evans settled into a stubborn partnership which lasted until about 40 minutes of the afternoon had gone. The gap between the scores was not yet alarming but it was beginning to concern us about how much time we were going to have. And there was always the danger that it might rain again. Just one more shower would have killed off any chance we might have had. For some time, Brian Close had been dropping hints (in the ponderous way that only he could) about having a bowl and eventually I gave him the ball. What happened next was, I suppose, typical of the way Brian played his cricket – the first ball was a long hop and was despatched for four. The next eight produced three wickets and no further runs! Glamorgan were all out for 101 – exactly our first innings score, so we now needed 66 to win and plenty of time to get them – if it didn't rain! We had a nasty shock straight away.

Jeff Jones, the left-arm fast bowler who was at that time knocking on the door of the Test selectors (he was picked the following year) had taken the wickets of Don Wilson and Mel Ryan in two balls to finish off our first innings. He now bowled Ken Taylor, who had batted so well in our first innings, with the first ball of the second. It was a pretty unusual hat-trick, spread over two innings and three days. But it was just the start we did not want. However, with John Hampshire standing firm at one end, Sharpe, Close and Stott cobbled together the necessary runs and we actually won with two hours to spare. It was Yorkshire's championship and I couldn't have retired on a happier note.

But is is difficult to forget that wasted second day and the suspense of wondering whether we would ever get the ground fit for play on the third. It was remarkable that none of the 5,000 crowd seemed to want to go home, even though the ground was becoming more water-logged by the minute. When the popular pork pies from Oliver's arrived for sale in Bolland's Bar, which Dennis Braithwaite was running, I'm told they were grabbed, hot from the butcher's tray, and eaten before they ever reached the counter. No one wanted to waste a minute which could be used for mopping-up operations. And without those splendid people who got out their gardening tools to help drain away the surface water, how could the ground have ever been made fit for play?

One way and another, it was a classic example of Yorkshiremen giving a helping hand to each other to win another championship.

GLAMORGAN

First Innings		Second Innings	
W.G.A. Parkhouse lbw b Ryan	0	lbw b Illingworth	9
B. Hedges b Wilson	13	lbw b Wilson	13
A. Jones c Sharpe b Wilson	11	c Close b Wilson	9
A.R. Lewis lbw b Illingworth	0	c Wilson b Illingworth	17
P. Walker c Stott b Wilson	6	c Sharpe b Wilson	14
J. Pressdee c and b Wilson	15	lbw b Illingworth	8
D.J. Ward c Wilson JV b Illingworth	4	not out	19
D.L. Evans not out	6	c Sharpe b Close	8
D.J. Shepherd c and b Wilson	5	c Taylor b Wilson	0
O.S. Wheatley c Wilson JV b Illingworth	3	c and b Close	0
I.J. Jones c Close b Wilson	0	b Close	0
Extras	2	Extras	4
Total	65	Total	101

YORKSHIRE

First Innings		Second Innings	
K. Taylor c Evans b Shepherd	67	b Jones	0
J.H. Hampshire b Ward	4	not out	24
P.J. Sharpe c Jones b Ward	13	c Lewis b Shepherd	12
D.B. Close run out	0	c and b Ward	13
W.B. Stott b Wheatley	5	not out	9
R. Illingworth lbw b Wheatley	0	)	
J.V. Wilson b Wheatley	8	)	
F.S. Trueman b Wheatley	8	) did not bat	
D. Wilson c Evans b Jones	1	)	
J.G. Binks not out	0	)	
M. Ryan b Jones	0	)	
Extras	2	Extras	8
Total	101	Total (for 3 wkts)	66

Bowling
GLAMORGAN (first innings): Trueman 6-3-7-0; Ryan 4-2-4-1; Illingworth 21-8-28-3; Wilson D 19.3-10-24-6; (second innings): Trueman 11-6-15-0; Ryan 3-2-1-0; Illingworth 27-16-29-3; Wilson D 31-17-48-4; Close 1.3-0-4-3.
YORKSHIRE (first innings): Jones 2.3-0-6-2; Wheatley 17-9-21-4; Shepherd 24-15-35-1; Ward 9-1-37-2; (second innings): Jones 2-1-9-1; Wheatley 5-1-10-0; Shepherd 7.1-2-19-1; Ward 4-0-20-1.

13

John Hampshire

Glamorgan v Yorkshire
Cardiff 1963
24th, 25th, 26th July

JOHN HARRY HAMPSHIRE, *born Thurnscoe, 10.2.1941. Right-hand batsman, leg-break bowler. Scored 1,000 runs in a season 15 times and averaged 53.20 in 1978. Scored 107 in his first Test innings which was at Lord's (he was the first England batsman to do that) after going in at 61-4 against the West Indies. Captained Yorkshire in 1979 and 1980 and had a brief career (37 matches) with Derbyshire. An outstanding coach, he has also become one of England's top Test umpires and national coach in Zimbabwe.*

This was a great game played at the old Cardiff Arms Park, on what is now the Cardiff RFC ground, with the international rugby pitch on the other side of the main stand. For the best part of two days it had gone well with Yorkshire declaring at 332 for seven, and then Tony Nicholson making a dramatic break-through at the start of Glamorgan's first innings. For most of the second day the Welshmen played a stubborn rearguard action on a slow turner on which bowlers of all kinds really had to work for their wickets.

Don Wilson had five victims. Raymond, for once, had no reward other than a string of maidens – and he loved maiden overs almost as much as taking wickets. Few bowlers have hated to be hit as much as Raymond. When we finally claimed the last wicket Glamorgan were only 88 and there was no question of whether or not the follow-on should be enforced. This time there was no break-through at the top of the order and it promised to be harder work than ever. Runs didn't matter so much to Glamorgan as the consumption of time and so, on *that* pitch, they were not going to have *too* much of a struggle if they got their heads down and concentrated. It was a run out which did the trick, my return from, I think, long leg, just beating Bernie Hedges trying for an extra run.

But Wilson and Illingworth had had pretty long spells during the day and had now been in action for a fair time in the second innings. Spinning-fingers were feeling a bit sore, feet were tender and concentration was difficult. Still, it was a bit of a shock when Illy tossed the ball to me – he was captain in the absence of Close, on Test duty at Headingley. I had certainly developed as a youngster who bowled leg-spinners and batted at No.11 but at the age of 14, making my first appearance for Rotherham Town second team, I had been offered a promotion to No.9 by the captain. At that time I certainly didn't think in terms of playing for Yorkshire, but I could *hope*, like most lads of my age. There was an unspoken, unwritten, unmentioned tradition in Yorkshire that leg-break bowlers were regarded with suspicion, whichever side they played for, and at 14 I had already begun to reckon that I might have a bit more future as a batsman!

It was certainly as a batsman that I had been called up by Yorkshire and though at that time I was not capped, I spent most of 1963 opening with Duggie Padgett. My leg-spinning was not taken seriously in the side, nor did I expect it to be. I had bowled one over at Taunton that season and four against Gloucs – nett result, none for 37 – all in circumstances which were certainly not serious. Yet to have a go now made reasonable cricketing sense. Slow bowling was more likely to put the brake on scoring than the quicker stuff and we had to invite the opposition to lose patience. We had runs to play with and the pitch *was* a turner, even if a slow one. It worked.

My first wicket was, I think, that of Alan Rees, a rugby international who had turned pro with Leeds, who was caught at slip and I bowled Alwyn Harris, a left-hander. As we left the field, Illy told me I would be opening the bowling next morning. There was quite a bit of chat in the hotel that night . . .

Next morning I arrived earlier than usual and put in a bit of practice; Illy offered me his treasured Friar's Balsam to anoint my spinning finger. The rest is history. Wilson took one wicket and I got the remaining five. The game was over by a quarter to twelve and we were in Worcester for the next game by the time one of our travelling Pressmen arrived at the Cardiff ground to find the gates closed. Did I bowl a googly? Let me put it this way: one of my clean-bowled victims positioned himself for the leg-break and was bowled *off his box!*

I must confess to a feeling of disappointment that "Hampshire: 7-52" has never been recorded in the Yorkshire Year Book under "exceptional bits of bowling" but the figures cannot be disputed, just the same. I do enjoy asking modern bowlers what their best figures are and waiting for the reciprocal question? "What were yours?" It's good to be able to consider for a moment and then to toss out airily, "Let me see now . . . best figures . . . er . . . I think that would be at Cardiff in 1963 . . . seven for 52."

It's remarkable how many people that causes to shut up!

Now in most other counties that performance would have earned a player a bit of professional respect. You might think he would have been used frequently in later games as a front-line bowler. At the very worst, it merited being called up occasionally as a sort of secret weapon. But that, I have to say with some sadness and a passing thought of what-might-have-been, was not the case. Over the next 18 years I was permitted – grudgingly, I thought – to add 17 more scalps to my belt and never can I recall being regarded as a potential matchwinner.

Still, seven for 52, it's a nice memory to have. And no Yorkshire bowler can ever do it again at Cardiff Arms Park. It's a full-time rugby ground.

YORKSHIRE

First Innings

D.E.V. Padgett run out	28
J.H. Hampshire lbw b Pressdee	80
R.A. Hutton c Evans b Shepherd	31
W.B. Stott c Walker b Wheatley	66
G. Boycott c Pressdee b Shepherd	80
D. Wilson c Hedges b Wheatley	25
R. Illingworth b Wheatley	14
J.G. Binks not out	0
M. Ryan)	
A.G. Nicholson) did not bat	
R.K. Platt)	
Extras	7
Total (for 7 wkts dec)	332

GLAMORGAN

First Innings		Second Innings	
B. Hedges b Nicholson	7	run out	16
A. Jones lbw b Nicholson	4	c Boycott b Wilson	28
A. Harris c Illingworth b Wilson	16	b Hampshire	43
A. Rees b Nicholson	11	c Hutton b Hampshire	31
J.S. Pressdee c Wilson b Ryan	4	c Illingworth b Wilson	2
P. Walker not out	20	b Hampshire	9
F.J. Davis run out	0	b Hampshire	10
D.L. Evans c Binks b Wilson	18	c Hutton b Hampshire	13
D.J. Shepherd b Wilson	0	c sub b Hampshire	6
O.S. Wheatley c Ryan b Wilson	0	c Binks b Hampshire	9
I.J. Jones c Hutton b Wilson	0	not out	7
Extras	8	Extras	7
Total	88	Total	178

Bowling
YORKSHIRE: Jones 19-8-52-0; Wheatley 28-8-86-3; Walker 5-1-23-0; Shepherd 37.2-17-61-2; Pressdee 26-6-78-1; Davis 9-4-25-0.
GLAMORGAN (first innings): Nicholson 14-7-20-3; Ryan 10-5-9-1; Platt 7-3-11-0; Wilson 18.5-8-33-5; Illingworth 10-7-7-0; (second innings): Nicholson 12-2-29-0; Ryan 8-0-18-0; Wilson 31-15-51-2; Illingworth 17-9-21-0; Hampshire 13-2-52-7.

14

Geoffrey Boycott

Middlesex v Yorkshire
Lord's 1963
17th, 19th, 20th August

G EOFFREY BOYCOTT, OBE, *born 21.10.1940, Fitzwilliam. Outstanding right-hand opening bat, occasional medium-pace in-swing bowler. A player whose determination to succeed made him unique, Boycott twice averaged 100 or more in a season and played in well over 100 Tests for England. In 1981 he became the highest-scoring batsman in Test history, up to that time. In 563 completed innings for Yorkshire between 1962 and 1986 he scored 32,570 runs at an average of 57.85. He was captain from 1971 to 1978.*

Although Geoffrey Boycott has not contributed to this book, the editor felt it appropriate to include an outstanding match for him here.

Saturday, 17th August, 1963, was a miserable day in London. It rained all day. The players hung about the dressing-rooms at Lord's, playing cards, doing crossword puzzles, reading newspapers and going through all those little chores which the weather sometimes forces upon cricketers everywhere. On Sunday, they went off to play golf at the friendly and hospitable club at Finchley where, as usual, they were given the courtesy of the course.

At the same time, there were nervous glances at the skies because once more Yorkshire were in contention for the county championship with only three more games to play after that one and some unlikely challengers snapping at their heels – Glamorgan, Somerset and Sussex.

Boycott was still only a Colt, an uncapped player. He had forced his way into the senior side the previous year with his heavy scoring for the Second XI and had re-appeared early in 1963, batting at No.6 in the opening match and failing to make any impact. He played again before the end of May, making only 9 as an opener against Gloucs at Bradford, and faring somewhat better (28 and 21 not out) at No.7 against Kent at Gravesend.

Boycott was a seriously depressed young man at this time – yearning to be given a chance to show just what he could do as a batsman yet unable to break through the barrier of seniority in the pecking order. Ranged ahead of him was the experience of Sharpe, Taylor, Padgett, Close, Stott, and Illingworth and his great rival, John Hampshire, invariably got precedence over him when it came to the last batting place. Even when Bolus left at the end of the 1962 season to join Nottinghamshire, a new threat appeared in the form of Richard Hutton during the summer vacations at Cambridge University.

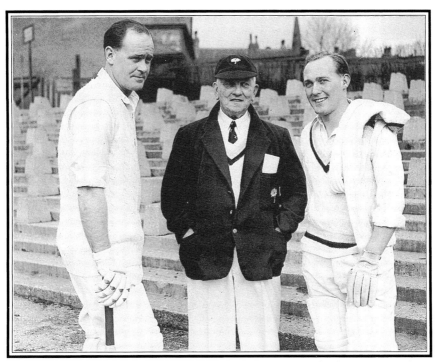

Brian Close, Maurice Leyland (coach) and Bryan Stott at Headingley in 1960. (Photo by Telegraph & Argus, Bradford)

Boycott waited in the wings, fretting in an agony of frustration. His chance came at last in, of all fixtures, the Roses match. He joined Bryan Stott, at No.5 in the order, with a scoreboard which read 56-3. Stott, in fact, played a considerable part in nursing his less-experienced partner through the start of his innings, and they were not parted until the board showed 305-4. Yorkshire won the game by an innings and 110 runs before lunch on the third day and the 22-year-old Boycott had made 145 – a maiden first-class century in his first Roses match. Nothing could have been sweeter.

He now stayed in the senior side, scoring pretty consistently but usually in the middle order. Skipper Close, however, had noted the youngster's well-organised defensive technique and had discussed with his lieutenants (Illingworth and Binks) the possibility that Boycott would make a sound opener. Nothing would suit Geoffrey better! He opened with John Hampshire against Warwickshire at Scarborough, scoring 62 and 28, and again at Old Trafford in the return Roses fixture where his 113 (and 20 not out) gave him the prize of a century in both games against Lancashire in one season – before he had been capped.

And so to his first appearance in a game at Lord's where he would again open the Yorkshire innings ... if the rain ever stopped. It rained again on Monday and ultimately Yorkshire found themselves having to bat on a seriously rain-affected wicket. The ball kicked and reared without any semblance of consistency. Moss and Price, the opening pair, were followed by Bennett and Hooker, medium-fast seamers who could not have asked for more help from the pitch. Titmus, the off-spinner, was not called up until the very latest stages.

Boycott lost his opening partner, Hampshire, without a run on the board. Sharpe followed at 32 (most of them scored by Boycott), Close at 46, Padgett at 47 and Illingworth at 86. Still the young man from Fitzwilliam battled on, showing a marvellously mature technique. It was a bad-wicket innings his two illustrious predecessors, Herbert Sutcliffe and Len Hutton, would have been proud to call their own.

It's a bit difficult to recall how many utterly unplayable deliveries Boycott managed, somehow, to cope with or to let go through – but there were an awful lot of them. Eventually he got one that even he couldn't cope with – a ball from Moss which hit the seam, moved away from the defensive bat and really took off. Murray took the catch and Boycott was just ten runs short of a century on his first appearance at Lord's – on the most difficult pitch he was likely to see again for a long time.

YORKSHIRE

First Innings

J.H. Hampshire lbw b Moss	0
G. Boycott c Murray b Moss	90
P.J. Sharpe c Parfitt b Price	6
D.B.Close c Murray b Price	9
D.E.V. Padgett c Murray b Bennett	0
R. Illingworth lbw b Price	12
R.A. Hutton run out	6
F.S. Trueman c Murray b Bennett	16
J.G. Binks c Murray b Titmus	0
D. Wilson not out	4
A.G. Nicholson b Bennett	0
Extras	1
Total	144

MIDDLESEX

First Innings

W.E. Russell b Nicholson	20
S.E. Russell c Sharpe b Nicholson	18
P.H. Parfitt c Binks b Nicholson	38
R.A. White lbw b Trueman	2
R.W. Hooker lbw b Nicholson	11
F.J. Titmus c Hutton b Trueman	9
E.A. Clark c Binks b Nicholson	11
J.T. Murray not out	24
D. Bennett b Trueman	1
J.S. Price not out	0
A.E. Moss did not bat	
Extras	11
Total (for 8 wkts)	145

Bowling
YORKSHIRE: Moss 16-7-22-2; Price 16-1-48-3; Bennett 15.5-3-43-3; Hooker 10-3-26-0; Titmus 2-1-4-1.
MIDDLESEX : Trueman 30.4-8-66-3; Nicholson 35-14-43-5; Hutton 8-2-23-0; Wilson 3-1-2-0.

15

Jimmy Binks

Middlesex v Yorkshire
Lord's 1964
10th, 11th, 12th June

JAMES GRAHAM BINKS, *born 5.10.1935, Hull. Right-hand batsman, wicketkeeper. Jimmy Binks played 491 matches for Yorkshire but, outstandingly, he kept wicket in 412 consecutive county championship matches for the county between 1955 and 1969. He toured Ceylon, India and Pakistan with MCC in 1961-62. To the astonishment of most people in the game he played only twice for England – on the tour of India in 1963-64 when he opened the batting in Calcutta with another Yorkshireman, Brian Bolus. Now lives in the USA where he is the West Coast representative for a firm of hydraulics systems manufacturers.*

Wicket-keeping records are very nice to have and it is good to have set one or two. Personal wicket-keeping rivalries can evoke a few memories, too. One of those clearest in my mind is when I was given out, stumped by Alan Knott, when I knew perfectly well that I wasn't out at all. But it's said that these things even themselves out over a career in the game and in that particular one, when it was Kent's turn to bat. I appealed for a stumping against Knottie and the square-leg umpire signalled "Out". He wasn't, actually. The same umpire had made two mistakes in the same game – he went on to become a Test umpire – and it was quite nice to feel that things had evened themselves out rather quickly.

But wicket-keeping was, after all, my job. I can't think there has ever been a cricketer who didn't want to succeed in a role in which he was not regarded as a specialist. I was no different from anyone else, and I yearned for a record as a batsman. It's not easy to make runs when you spend your career down at eight to 11 in the order (No.7, just occasionally if one was lucky) and especially it wasn't easy at all in the Yorkshire team of the 1950s and 1960s. Quite a lot of good players went in before me. But I got close to a century at least twice – quite close – but the closer I got, the more cruel fate dogged me. When I got closest of all, cruel fate appeared in the person of one of the distinguished authors of this book . . .

Simply getting to three figures would have been enough to satisfy me but the unkindest cut of all was to get within striking distance, twice, and on both occasions it was at Lord's. In the first game of the 1963 season, against MCC at headquarters, I got to 88 in a match eventually ruined by rain, and that seemed destined to stand as my career-best until June the following year when we played Middlesex and they declared at 279 for nine. On the second day we slumped to 82-5, then 101-6. My hour had come. With Chris Balderstone – the Colt and the 'keeper – 126 runs were added for the next wicket. Chris was out for 58 and then Don Wilson helped add another 33 runs but

Richard Hutton and father Sir Leonard, former England and Yorkshire opener, at Huddersfield in 1968 before Yorkshire took on an International XI. (Photo by Telegraph & Argus, Bradford)

we still hadn't managed a first-innings lead which, in 1964, meant two points. Enter F.S. Trueman...

Fred *had* a certain reputation with the bat and very proud he was of it, too. He already had a first-class century to his credit – against Northants the previous year – and I don't think he was terribly happy at finding himself at No.10 in the Yorkshire batting order. But he

settled down with a lordly air of seniority and gradually we built up
the score ... first the lead, then we began to build on it. I saw my score
creep up to 95 and only a man of stone would have been able to resist
the thought of a century – at Lord's! – creeping into his mind at
that stage.

I was standing at the non-striker's end; a ball hit Fred on the pads
and ran away, down towards fine leg. There was a comfortable run ...
I called ... and started. No response. I called again ... and ventured a
bit further. No response. Fred was surveying the scene, a bit like W.G.
must have done when he knew he was on the way to yet another
hundred against mere mortal opposition.

I tried again. No response. So I set off, thinking it might produce
some reaction, I reached the other end and was mildly surprised to find
my partner still taking no immediate interest in proceedings. He didn't
even look at me as we stood in the same crease. I thought the situation
might have called for some sort of comment if it had only been,
"Hello, Sunshine. What are you doing here?" But ... nothing. The ball
had been gathered and the fielder was preparing to throw.

I thought I had better try to get back to the other end. I ran like
hell ... desperately I raced along the pitch. In the space of a few
seconds I had covered 40 yards or so. And I was run out by one yard.

Even the opposition – keen as they were to avoid a big first-innings
deficit – were on my side. Those who weren't rolling about on the
ground laughing were profuse in their offerings of sympathy. Fred
gazed dispassionately into the middle distance as the umpire signalled
that I was run out ... for 95 ... at Lord's!

There were other disappointments in my career – that cannot be
denied. Even those golden days when I captained Yorkshire (in the
absence of Close, Trueman and Illingworth) had their downbeat
moments – like the time we had two overs to get three runs and didn't
get them – but I just can't recall one as bad as that on 11th June,
1964. Run out on 95. It could, I suppose, have been just a bit worse.
I might have got to 99. And *then* what would I have said to FS?

MIDDLESEX

First Innings		Second Innings	
W.E. Russell b Trueman	8	lbw b Wilson	17
R.A. Gale lbw b Wilson	41	b Illingworth	6
P.H. Parfitt c and b Wilson	73	b Illingworth	8
R.W. Hooker b Illingworth	4	b Wilson	31
E.A. Clark b Wilson	0	c Balderstone b Wilson	7
F.J. Titmus c Padgett b Illingworth	7	c Sharpe b Balderstone	4
J.T. Murray c Binks b Wilson	72	c Close b Illingworth	0
M.J. Smith c Padgett b Trueman	20	not out	6
D. Bennett c Taylor b Trueman	46	lbw b Balderstone	13
C.D. Drybrough not out	0	not out	4
J.S. Price did not bat		did not bat	
Extras	8	Extras	–
Total (for 9 wkts dec)	279	Total (for 8 wkts)	96

YORKSHIRE

First Innings	
K. Taylor c Drybrough b Titmus	56
J.H. Hampshire lbw b Bennett	8
D.E.V. Padgett c Russell b Hooker	22
D.B. Close d Drybrough b Titmus	7
P.J. Sharpe c and b Hooker	1
R. Illingworth lbw b Titmus	2
J.C. Balderstone lbw b Titmus	58
J.G. Binks run out	95
D. Wilson b Hooker	15
F.S. Trueman b Bennett	54
M. Ryan not out	2
Extras	11
Total	331

Bowling
MIDDLESEX (first innings): Trueman 22.3-4-64-3; Ryan 14-1-39-0; Close 11-3-38-0; Illingworth 36-14-48-2; Wilson 36-13-76-4; Balderstone 5-4-6-0; (second innings): Trueman 4-1-13-0; Ryan 2-1-5-0; Illingworth 25-11-46-3; Wilson 20-13-19-3; Balderstone 9-5-9-2; Close 2-1-4-0.
YORKSHIRE: Price 26-5-55-0; Bennett 16.2-3-46-2; Titmus 49-17-85-4; Drybrough 21-7-36-0; Gale 5-1-13-0; Booker 30-6-78-3; Parfitt 5-1-7-0.

16

Ken Taylor

Yorkshire v Surrey
Bradford 1964
27th, 29th, 30th June

K ENNETH TAYLOR, *born 21.8.1935, Huddersfield. Right-hand batsman, right-arm medium-pace bowler, outstanding fieldsman, especially in the covers or deep. Played 303 matches for Yorkshire between 1953 and 1968 and in three Tests for England; soccer for Huddersfield Town and Bradford and was reserve for both the England B and Under-23 teams in the days when substitutes were not allowed. Thus he just missed an international cricket and football "double" like another Huddersfield man, Willie Watson. He played first-class cricket and coached in New Zealand and in South Africa where he also coached soccer. A gifted artist, he studied at the Slade and, with his wife Avril, now runs the Art Department at Beeston Hall preparatory school in Norfolk where Ken also handles physical education and coaches cricket and soccer.*

Editor's Note: Although Ken Taylor scored nearly 13,000 runs for Yorkshire with 16 centuries and hit 1,000 runs or more in a season on six occasions, it was not simply as a batsman that he made his mark. He had a highest score of 203 not out against Warwickshire in 1961 and was particularly proud of his 160 against the touring Australians in 1964 – the highest this century by a Yorkshireman in a Yorkshire v Australia game. His medium-paced bowling earned him 131 wickets, usually in the context of breaking a stubborn partnership, but neither is that the way most people remember him. The outstanding characteristic of Ken Taylor's cricket had to be his magnificent athleticism in the field. His team-mates reckoned that with Taylor in the covers and Don Wilson at mid-wicket they could save between 40 and 50 runs in an innings and over their full careers that adds up to an awful lot of runs saved.

Taylor held 150 catches for Yorkshire (one for England) which does not seem an especially high figure compared with Close's 811 and Sharpe's 615. But they both fielded close to the wicket where most catches occur; Taylor was almost always in the deep where a fielder often has to make a lot of ground to complete a catch. And that is why, in asking him to recall one particular match, we suggested he might remember a catch which still lingers in his mind.

The best catch I think I ever took was at Park Avenue, Bradford, on Monday, 29th June, 1964, during a match against Surrey. Perhaps I might simply give the details and not labour the point. It is not for me to say too much about any achievement of mine but this one really does linger in the mind, perhaps because it was a rather important one for Yorkshire at that particular time.

Whilst I was usually positioned in the covers, on this occasion I had been placed well back between deep mid-wicket and long on. A big partnership had developed between Mickey Stewart and Ken Barrington which had already realised 144 runs and Surrey looked like getting a big first innings lead. Ray Illingworth was bowling and had come in for a bit of stick from Barrington who was, of course, a fine player of off-spin. Ray hated to be "collared" by any batsman, and in fact very rarely was, but Barrington was such a good player off his legs that we couldn't do much about it. He was going really well. When he had reached 76 and obviously had a hundred in mind, he went for a straight six towards the pavilion and where the white-painted brick wall stood in front of the members' seats.

Illy, on the other hand, was always thinking, always scheming, always plotting a batsman's downfall no matter how well-set he seemed. How this ball differed from the others is something perhaps only Ray could tell us but it soared high in the air. One minute it looked certain to land amongst the members, the next it seemed there might just possibly be a ghost of a chance of intercepting it. This collection of jumbled thoughts swirled in my mind as I set off to my left, not *really* expecting to get there. As I raced across the ground the ball was coming down and I thought I might as well give it a go. I jumped, as high as I could, and flung up my left arm. To my surprise, the ball hit my hand and stuck; I clung to it as I came down to earth.

Now there are a number of reasons why I remember the occasion so well. Illy, not the most demonstrative of men, nearly trampled me underfoot in his delight. Ken Barrington, a lovely man, used to mention the catch every time we met after that until his sad and untimely death in the West Indies in 1981.

I must say I enjoyed all aspects of fielding; it was exhilarating to be involved in the chasing, retrieving, catching or throwing. It can have its rewards, too. At Sheffield, in 1964, the Milk Marketing Board sponsored a throwing contest at the end of a day's play in the match against the tourists and I won it with a throw of 112 yards. The first prize was £25 and Avril and I spent it on a weekend at Bamburgh. It just about covered the cost of the holiday for two of us!

On the other hand, there was a great temptation to choose Harrogate, 1962, when the invitation came to select a match I remembered well. Everyone I meet seems to remember that I was Jeff Jones' last victim in the hat-trick which was spread over the two innings. What *I* like to remember is that my first-innings score of 67 was two runs more than the total of the entire Glamorgan team and more than half the Yorkshire total. As the runs were scored on a wet pitch which seamed and turned from the start I think any batsman would look back with affection on a decent score in such circumstances.

Harrogate, I suppose, figures in a lot of our memories. Vic Wilson (as he tells elsewhere) led Yorkshire to their 1962 championship win there and went into honourable retirement. Yorkshire had several notable and significant victories there, in fact, but we had one or two laughs there as well.

I remember the time when Peter West arrived to cover a game for *The Times*. The previous evening he had been thrust by the BBC into a televised debate on the old North v South theme and as far as most of the players and crowd were concerned that day, he had been on the "wrong" side. Peter was also presenter of the TV programme "Come Dancing", a job which, as a freelance broadcaster, he was naturally glad to have but it took a bit of living down when he moved from the ballroom to the sporting arena. Now, with the previous night's remarks in mind (we were in the field), players and crowd started up a rhythmic chanting, "One-two-three, one-two-three," as he walked half the distance round the ground from entrance to pavilion. Peter was acutely embarrassed but he managed a brave smile as the chanting followed him all the way to the press box.

There were a lot of smiles, too, on the occasion when Fred called for the pitch to be measured after his first few deliveries on a slow, wet pitch had struggled to reach the other end at the start of a game at St. George's Road.

Champagne celebrations in the dressing room after winning the championship in 1962. (Photo by Telegraph & Argus, Bradford)

He didn't win that one because the pitch was solemnly re-measured and found, indeed, to be precisely 22 yards in length but Fred didn't have too many bad days. To my mind he was the greatest quick bowler we have seen and when I close my eyes and think back to the 1960s the first image I see is FS in full flight from the pavilion end at Bradford, expecting a wicket with every ball and looking disappointed if he didn't get it. He would bowl with as much enthusiasm at half-past five as he had done at half-past eleven and he never wanted to let the ball out of his hands.

It was a great time to be a Yorkshireman and in particular a Yorkshire cricketer. It was a privilege to be in that side.

YORKSHIRE

First Innings		Second Innings	
G. Boycott run out	46	c Stewart b Harman	15
K. Taylor c Willett b Sydenham	80	c and b Harman	16
D.E.V. Padgett c Long b Harman	8	lbw b Tindall	20
D.B. Close b Harman	0	not out	100
P.J. Sharpe c Barrington b Harman	12	c and b Gibson	44
R. Illingworth c Gibson b Tindall	2	c Long b Gibson	0
J.H. Hampshire lbw b Sydenham	80	c Barrington b Harman	3
D. Wilson c and b Tindall	11	b Storey	25
J.G. Binks b Tindall	4	c Edrich b Harman	0
F.S. Trueman b Sydenham	12	lbw b Harman	50
M. Ryan not out	3	b Barrington	5
Extras	15	Extras	14
Total	273	Total	292

SURREY

First Innings	
M.J. Stewart c Taylor b Illingworth	130
J.H. Edrich c Sharpe b Wilson	19
M.J. Edwards c Close b Illingworth	1
K.F. Barrington c Taylor b Illingworth	76
M. Willett b Illingworth	19
R.A.E. Tindall st Binks b Ryan	34
S.J. Storey c Binks b Trueman	40
D. Gibson c Sharpe b Trueman	12
A. Long not out	3
R. Harman lbw b Trueman	0
D.A.D. Sydenham c Taylor b Trueman	15
Extras	9
Total	358

Bowling
YORKSHIRE (first innings): Sydenham 24.2-6-54-3; Gibson 25-9-38-0; Storey 5-0-22-0; Harman 31-11-122-3; Tindall 13-4-22-3; (second innings): Sydenham 12-2-35-0; Gibson 23-7-35-2; Harman 38-15-99-5; Tindall 29-14-61-1; Barrington 8.4-0-26-1; Storey 8-1-17-1; Willett 4-0-5-0.
SURREY (first innings): Trueman 15.3-3-45-4; Ryan 10-1-29-1; Illingworth 35-5-134-4; Wilson 33-10-98-1; Close 11-0-43-0.

17

Richard Hutton

Yorkshire v Lancashire
Headingley 1964
1st, 3rd, 4th August

R ICHARD ANTHONY HUTTON, *born 6.9.1942, Pudsey. Middle order right-hand batsman, right-arm fast-medium bowler. Blue in all his three years at Cambridge University, 1962-64. Five Tests for England in 1971. Played 208 matches for Yorkshire between 1962 and 1974, scoring just under 5,000 runs and taking nearly 500 wickets. Son of Sir Leonard Hutton, he had an earlier career in banking and is now Editorial Director of The Cricketer.*

Playing cricket for Yorkshire in the 1960s is an experience more easily remembered than described. Having already represented Surrey at second eleven level – and in the 1950s Surrey and Yorkshire were tigers at each other's throats – I found myself in the incongruous position of travelling solo on a train from Euston Station to Manchester Piccadilly to join a Yorkshire team, most of whom I had never met before, for the traditional August Bank Holiday Roses Match.

The strength of Yorkshire cricket at the turn of the 50s was such that as I headed north many less fortunate Yorkshire-born cricketers were heading south. This exodus gathered pace and by the mid-60s Leicestershire, for example, was almost a Yorkshire second eleven.

The Yorkshire team of the 1960s was like no other team on earth. It consisted for a time of 13 players – capped ones. Never, before or since, can so many highly talented, competitive and individualistic men have been so successfully grouped together. Composed as it was of professionals playing as professionals and amateurs playing as professionals, every attribute of human nature was represented. The team was driven and held together in the knowledge that it embodied the great traditions of Yorkshire cricket, that it was in the natural line of succession to some of the greatest names in cricket, and in response to a public having high expectations.

Against this background my Yorkshire career began on an early August Saturday morning in a state of much trepidation. I am not choosing this particular match as my most memorable, but it remains strong in the mind and as a result my remembrance of Roses cricket in the 1960s eventually became an affectionate one.

After a night without sleep I was engaged by the Yorkshire captain, Vic Wilson, at the breakfast table in a discussion about my effectiveness in bowling at left-handers. Apparently F.S. Trueman had an aversion, comparatively speaking, to left-handers, and Lancashire had plenty of them, all the way down to the bowlers. Naively, at the time, I saw not much difference between left- and right-handers, which probably explains why so much of my bowling to left-handers went down the leg side.

Arriving at Old Trafford, I had never seen so many people at a sporting venue. Almost 15,000 were inside and there was still an hour to go before the start. Entering the Yorkshire dressing-room and at the same time trying to stay invisible, the self-styled 'greatest fast bowler ever to draw breath' was holding centre stage. A semi-clad figure, to use the term loosely (covered as it was in nothing other than a Yorkshire cap, jock-strap, socks and cricket boots with ankles reaching mid calf and studs the length and strength of two-inch nails), was surveying the scene through the dressing-room window with a pair of high-powered binoculars. A growl issued from between teeth clutching a giant pipe: "This is the worst bloody crowd I've ever seen at a Roses match."

Fortunately much of the match was spent sheltering from the weather, but not before I had incurred the great bowler's wrath by failing to hold on to a swirling ball at deep third man off a steepling hit from the outside edge of a tailender's bat. Such are events etched in the memory.

FS, deputising for an injured Brian Close, led Yorkshire to one of the county's finest achievements in the 1960s – the innings defeat of Australia at Bramall Lane, the county's first victory against Australia since 1902. Quite rightly this qualifies for consideration, but my own part in it was modest enough. It was an outstanding team effort, but it did provide me with one of the most exciting moments of my cricketing life, and a welcome relief from spending most of the match posted at deep square-leg, grovelling around on all fours to cling on to mishit sweeps from the bowling of Raymond Illingworth.

Having batted on in to the second day, our chance of winning the game came alive when Australia lost their first five wickets for 99, two of them to myself, both pouched by the aforementioned FS at slip. Further progress was impeded by the presence of Bill Lawry, whose batting style on that tour had been unflatteringly and unkindly likened to 'a corpse with pads on'. With number eleven at the crease Lawry, who had batted throughout the innings, surprised the world by getting out.

The day was a sweltering, sunless one of intense humidity. Overhead conditions were oppressive, so much so that those in the region prone to exaggeration reported that within a 40-mile radius of the ground great balls of red earth were falling from the sky. As Lawry left the field prior to starting Australia's second innings he signalled ominously his intentions by placing both his batting gloves on the ground, palms upward, to dry in the sun and to be retrieved on his way back.

After Fred had bowled the first over, my first ball of the second was an in-swinging yorker that clipped the base of Lawry's leg stump. The door was opened, and in the ensuing eruption I distinctly remember being congratulated by a Yorkshire player! Never had I felt so appreciated and the glowing sensation erased the lingering memory of a few weeks earlier of having been hit into the bowling greens at Park Avenue by Gary Sobers.

However, for my favourite match of the 60s I am returning to a Roses match, another August fixture, but this time at Headingley in 1964. The outcome was a substantial innings defeat for Lancashire in a match I often reflect on with much amusement.

Lancashire's team contained Sonny Ramadhin in his first year of a two-year contract with Lancashire. No longer quite the bowler he was 14 years earlier when he and Alf Valentine bowled West Indies to their first win in a Lord's Test match, he was still a tricky customer and bowling with his cap on and sleeves buttoned at the wrist, this diminutive figure retained an ability to deviate the ball both ways without easy detection by the batsman. Essentially he was an off-spinner with a leg-break that was cut rather than spun from the fingers, and it had a slightly higher trajectory than his normal delivery.

Yorkshire batsmen never much liked having to decide which way a ball was likely to deviate and accordingly tended to proceed with caution. So it was that having put out Lancashire for 101 by mid-afternoon on a Saturday in front of a substantial audience, Messrs Boycott and Sharpe remained intact for the remainder of the day concerned more with consolidation born of a suspicion of Ramadhin than with ramming home our advantage. These tactics caused the fearsome and vociferous Chairman of the Cricket Committee, Brian Sellers, to consider his responsibilities and at close of play, with the side feeling smugly satisfied with having all ten wickets in hand and within range of Lancashire's score on a pitch likely to become receptive to spin, he appeared in the dressing-room to deliver in terminology of which there was none superior, a castigation for slow batting and for failing to provide the watching public with value for their money.

The team possessed an accomplished mimic of the Cricket Chairman with an impersonation that went as far as the "prop" of a pair of half moon spectacles over which Sellers peered when getting his points across. As the chairman left the room (but before he realised the door was not fully closed) John Hampshire, having quickly grabbed his prop from his coat pocket, started to repeat the speech. Catching a whiff of it before the door closed, Sellers stuck his head round it and looking straight at John Hampshire, before finally retreating, uttered the immortal words, 'You pillock!'.

When we resumed after the weekend, again before a sizeable gathering, I found myself sitting on the pavilion balcony alongside Raymond Illingworth. He was due to bat at number six and I was next when Ramadhin began to take the earliest of his eight wickets. Even then Ray Illingworth knew more about the game than most of the side put together and from his own personal experience of Ramadhin on the 1960 MCC Tour of the West Indies he knew exactly how to deal with him.

"Whatever you do, don't play back," he advised.

"OK, Ray," I replied, taking comfort in the fact that I much preferred to play forward than back.

"Whatever you do, don't play back," he repeated.

I told him I understood what he was telling me, and immediately afterwards Boycott played back, was hit on the pad and given out lbw. Ray followed him in and to his first ball . . . played back, also to be struck on the pad and given out lbw.

There cannot be many less pleasurable ways of spending an August Bank Holiday Monday than walking out in front of 10,000 people against Lancashire to avert a Ramadhin hat trick. On my way I looked around for Illingworth to see if there were further instructions to be received. Contact was not possible as he made his way back in an ever widening radius. It was to be one of the many moments in my life when I have felt myself to be completely alone.

Following the guiding and underlying Yorkshire principle, "Do as I say, not as I do", I played so far forward to my first ball that I trapped it between the ground and my boot. The ball was returned to the bowler ravaged by deep stud marks, the first instance of ball-tampering with the foot. Thereafter Ramadhin, in the course of his 50-over stint, was not the force he had been, and after John Hampshire and I added 39 for the sixth wicket, Jimmy Binks and I shared a partnership of 118 for the seventh wicket, which set up our defeat of Lancashire by an innings and 131 runs by the first half-hour of the third morning.

My performance was greeted by the Chairman of Cricket with the award of my county cap, and once again we were back to the happy position of having 13 capped players!

LANCASHIRE

First Innings		Second Innings	
D.M. Green c Binks b Trueman	17	b Nicholson	11
D.R. Worsley c Binks b Trueman	8	b Nicholson	3
G. Pullar c Padgett b Illingworth	29	not out	33
K. Grieves lbw b Trueman	5	c Close b Illingworth	18
P. Marner c Wilson b Close	10	lbw b Nicholson	7
R. Entwistle c Padgett b Trueman	9	lbw b Trueman	2
J.B. Statham c Binks b Illingworth	4	b Close	21
K. Higgs run out	3	c Binks b Nicholson	3
K. Goodwin not out	2	c Close b Nicholson	1
K. Howard c Hutton b Illingworth	2	lbw b Nicholson	4
S. Ramadhin c Padgett b Illingworth	10	b Nicholson	0
Extras	2	Extras	17
Total	101	Total	120

YORKSHIRE

First Innings	
G. Boycott lbw b Ramadhin	62
P.J. Sharpe c Statham b Ramadhin	15
D.E.V. Padgett b Ramadhin	0
D.B. Close b Ramadhin	17
J.H. Hampshire c Green b Howard	51
R. Illingworth lbw b Ramadhin	0
R.A. Hutton b Ramadhin	64
J.G. Binks b Ramadhin	75
F.S. Trueman c Worsley b Howard	24
D. Wilson b Ramadhin	22
A.G. Nicholson not out	2
Extras	20
Total	352

Bowling

LANCASHIRE (first innings): Trueman 15-4-35-4; Nicholson 13-3-31-0; Close 9-3-20-1; Illingworth 7.4-4-9-4; Wilson 1-0-4-0; (second innings): Trueman 16-3-25-1; Nicholson 19.5-6-32-7; Wilson 9-6-15-0; Illingworth 14-7-25-1; Close 6-4-6-1.

YORKSHIRE: Statham 31-7-85-0; Higgs 41-17-65-0; Ramadhin 50.1-16-121-8; Howard 17-4-61-2.

18

Ray
Illingworth

Kent v Yorkshire
Dover 1964
19th, 20th, 21st August

RAYMOND ILLINGWORTH, CBE, *born 8.6.1932, Pudsey. Right-hand batsman, off-break bowler. After 17 years with Yorkshire, he joined Leicestershire and played a major part in the most successful years of that county's history. He also took over the England captaincy with remarkable success including winning the Ashes in Australia on the stormy 1970-1971 tour. A genuine all-round cricketer, he scored 24,134 runs, took 2,072 wickets and held 446 catches. Illingworth was also an outstanding cricket "brain" on the field and now his comments on BBC Television are wise, authoritative and to the point. Appointed England "supremo" in 1994.*

This was another championship year so every game, every point, counted. We didn't often play at Dover so we didn't quite know what sort of pitch to expect – except that we knew it wouldn't be a very good one... the sort that gives both batsmen and bowlers some sort of chance. But even we weren't prepared for what we found!

Fourteen wickets in a match is always nice to have, especially when they cost barely 100 runs. But far more satisfactory was the 135 runs I got in a game where no one else made more than 36 (and he was on our side, too!). Thirty wickets fell in the match for fewer than 500 runs so I had to do a bit of grafting.

Of course, we got an idea of what was on as soon as we saw the names on the Kent team-sheet. They had not included a bowler with any sort of pace at all. Their attack consisted of two left-arm spinners, an off-spinner and leg-break-googly bowler who was also an opening batsman. On the other hand, they had packed in so many batsman that at No.8 they had Alan Knott who was to make five Test hundreds and 17 first-class centuries in his career. After him, at No.9, came Peter Jones who was credited with 1,000 runs in a season on a couple of occasions.

Alan Dixon, at No.10, was an all-rounder who managed 1,000 runs in a season three times and at No.11 they had "Deadly" Underwood, certainly a front-line bowler for all his career but very much a man with batting ambitions – he was always the first to volunteer to be nightwatchman in the England side.

So we knew only too well what sort of pitch to expect. In contrast – being on a southern tour, of course – we had forces which were limited to some extent. In fact that was the only game in which George Raymond Bloom was picked to play for Yorkshire, though as a fieldsman he certainly saw a bit of service as 12th man. He was our No.8, batting after Jimmy Binks.

We made a horrible start, losing Philip Sharpe before he'd scored and the next three wickets were down in fairly quick time but Closey

Ray Illingworth with daughter Diane in 1969. (Photo by Telegraph & Argus, Bradford)

and I steadied things and then I had another partnership with Binks. It was a session in which you had to watch every ball very closely indeed. You could have no idea what it might do – shoot, kick, turn or a combination of two such eccentricities – anything might happen. So to score 135 gave me as much pleasure as, I think, any innings I ever played.

And a total of 256 was better than we had ever dreamed of getting, too. Right. Now it was Kent's turn to see how they liked the pitch they had provided. The man we had most to worry about at least in theory, was, of course, Colin Cowdrey, the man who played in 114 Tests and made 107 centuries in his first-class career. But to tell the truth we never, in all the time I played, let ourselves be unduly concerned about "Kipper". He certainly didn't enjoy batting against Yorkshire.

He loved to play with the bat just behind his pads and there were times when he used the pads much more than the bat. Indeed, seven years earlier at Edgbaston against the West Indies he had made 154 in a partnership of 411 with Peter May which left Sonny Ramadhin complaining (and he still complains to this day) that he was "kicked out of the game" by Colin. Since Sonny bowled 588 deliveries in that England second innings, most of them to May and Cowdrey, he was in a position to speak from experience.

But Closey and I, from an early date, had developed an anti-Cowdrey defence system. It was quite simple. Closey just took up one of his suicidal positions – this time at silly point – so Cowdrey had to think about the dangers of a bat-pad catch. He knew, as everyone else knew, that Closey wasn't worried about being hit by the ball. He had been hit too many times for anyone to be particularly concerned about it. Certainly Brian never appeared to be concerned! So, one way and another, Cowdrey didn't present the threat to us that he did to most sides. He once complained about Closey taking up that silly point position to which Brian tersely replied, "If you'd play right in your head I wouldn't be here." All the same, his first-innings dismissal gave me a great deal of satisfaction. He tried to get to the pitch of the ball (as I had done) but he hadn't, you might say, my nimble and athletic footwork! He was "done" in the air and stumped by about four yards! I really enjoyed that.

I bowled 47 overs in the match and, naturally, the figures gave me great satisfaction. But, it has to be said, nothing like the pleasure of making 135 runs on that pitch. The game was over in two days and, needless to say, the two quicker bowlers had a bit of a rest. Fred Trueman delivered just 44 balls (including two no-balls) and Mel Ryan a mere 24. But Mel had the gratifying figures of 4-3-1-1. Not bad for two days work!

YORKSHIRE

First Innings

K. Taylor b Underwood	18
P.J. Sharpe c Luckhurst b Dixon	0
D.E.V. Padgett c Fillary b Dixon	11
J.H. Hampshire c Cowdrey b Underwood	11
D.B. Close c Cowdrey b Fillary	36
R. Illingworth c Cowdrey b Underwood	135
J.G. Binks b Fillary	16
G.R. Bloom b Underwood	2
F.S. Trueman c Wilson b Dixon	0
D. Wilson c Cowdrey b Dixon	9
M. Ryan not out	15
Extras	3
Total	256

KENT

First Innings		**Second Innings**	
B.W. Luckhurst c Close b Ryan	0	b Illingworth	0
E.J. Fillary c Wilson b Illingworth	9	not out	28
D. Nicholls b Illingworth	3	c Bloom b Illingworth	7
M.C. Cowdrey st Binks b Illingworth	21	b Wilson	29
R.C. Wilson c Trueman b Illingworth	19	lbw b Illingworth	22
J.M. Prodger c Illingworth b Wilson	10	b Wilson	1
M.H. Denness lbw b Illingworth	22	st Binks b Illingworth	3
A. Knott c Close b Illingworth	0	b Illingworth	9
P.H. Jones b Illingworth	2	c Bloom b Illingworth	8
A.L. Dixon not out	2	c Hampshire b Illingworth	11
D.L. Underwood run out	0	st Binks b Wilson	9
Extras	9	Extras	16
Total	97	Total	146

Bowling
YORKSHIRE: Dixon 50-9-128-4; Underwood 43.3-19-76-4; P.H. Jones 9-2-21-0; Fillary 12-1-28-2.
KENT (first innings): Trueman 5-3-10-0; Ryan 3-2-1-1; Illingworth 18-3-49-7; Wilson 17-9-28-1; (second innings): Trueman 2-0-6-0; Ryan 1-1-0-0; Wilson 23.1-5-47-3; Illingworth 29-6-52-7; Close 6-0-25-0.

19

Chris
Balderstone

Kent v Yorkshire
Canterbury 1967
9th, 10th, 11th July

JOHN CHRISTOPHER BALDERSTONE, *born 16.11.1940,
*Longwood (Huddersfield). Middle-order right-hand bat, slow
left-arm bowler. Played 68 games for Yorkshire over the period
1961 and 1968 and often smilingly referred to himself as "the
oldest Colt in the game". He went on to play 260 matches for
Leicestershire between 1971 and 1983 and was twice capped for
England during that period. A talented footballer (like two other
Huddersfield men, Willie Watson and Ken Taylor), he played for
Huddersfield Town, Carlisle United, Queen of the South (Scottish
League) and Doncaster Rovers. Lives in Leicestershire and is a first-
class umpire.*

At first glance, my choice of a special memory of one first-class cricket
match for Yorkshire might seem strange in the extreme, I didn't bowl,
didn't take a catch, scored one run in the first innings and one not out
in the second. What, you may ask, perfectly reasonably, was so
memorable about that? Nothing... well, nothing very spectacular...
except that I was at the crease when the winning run was struck and it
completed a quite remarkable sporting week for me.

It started at 8am on Friday, 4th July, when I teed off at Carlisle Golf
Club and had a very satisfying round of 76. I drove home, had a
couple of hours in bed, then joined the other Carlisle United players
for a trip up the A74 to play a practice match against Airdrieonians
which we won 4-1. My scrapbook records that I scored a goal and
"made" another. I got to bed at 12.45am. It had been a long day. Next
morning, Saturday, I had permission to drive to Huddersfield to play
in the Sykes Cup Final for Paddock against Holmfirth at Fartown...
and we won. The next two days, 6th and 7th, were spent training with
Carlisle United because the Football League season was less than ten
days away and Yorkshire chose this moment to ask for my release for
a week to play against Kent (Wednesday, Thursday, Friday) and
Derbyshire (Saturday, Monday, Tuesday).

Our manager, Tim Ward (formerly of Derby County) agreed that I
could go for the first game but said, reluctantly, I couldn't be spared
for the second. There was nothing personal in this. Derby footballer
he might have been but he was actually a keen follower of cricket and
he regarded it as an honour to have one of his footballers asked to
play county cricket. But the league season *was* approaching and he
was anxious to get his team into shape.

So – I accepted for the Kent match only and started to work out
how to get to Canterbury for 10.30am on Wednesday. We had a full-
scale "friendly" the previous night at Brunton Park, Carlisle, against
Sheffield United!

I played in the match (we won 2-0) and some time later I learned that the Cumberland *Evening News* had commented kindly on my "immaculate passing" and also "a 30-yard shot which threatened to demolish one of the new goalposts". I did not see that when it was originally published because after the game there was just enough time for a quick bath and an even quicker meal before I caught the midnight train to Euston.

We arrived at some ungodly hour, between six and seven and I hadn't, to be honest, had much rest in my sleeper-berth. I "lay in" for about another half-hour once we had reached London before making my way across the city to catch another train, this time to Canterbury. We lost the toss so it was straight out into the field! My first innings was undistinguished because Alan Dixon was having one of his best days ever with his off-spinners and I was, I think, the third of his seven victims. Nevertheless, we needed to make only 99 to win in the fourth innings and just when I was beginning to think I might not be required, John Hampshire was out. I had got off the mark ... just ... when Duggie Padgett hit the winning run: 99-3, we had won by seven wickets and my crowded sporting week ended with my playing a part, however modest, in a game which helped to win another county championship. My round trip of 680 miles had been worthwhile.

The double life of a cricketer-footballer can be good, and rewarding, but it can also lead to a few complications. Towards the end of the 1975 season Leicestershire were making a late spurt towards the

Gillhouley, Sharpe, Illingworth, Bolus, Taylor, Stott, D. Wilson and Cowan head for the nets during the warm up to the championship winning 1962 season. (Photo by Telegraph & Argus, Bradford)

county's first-ever championship and we were playing Derbyshire at Queen's Park, Chesterfield. It was a game we had to win. But I had just joined Doncaster Rovers towards the tail-end of my footballing career and on the second evening of our cricket match I was required by Rovers to play in a match at home to Brentford. Now all might have been well if I had got out early but Leics couldn't afford to have me do that.

I was 50-odd not out at close of play. I scarcely heard my Leicestershire captain (Ray Illingworth) congratulate me as my Doncaster manager (Stan Anderson) shepherded me out to the fast car, virtually waiting with the engine running. Cricket had finished at 6.30pm; kick-off in Doncaster was at 7.30pm. We made it, through the traffic, and won the game. The following day Leics beat Derbyshire and thus won the county championship for the first time in the club's history.

It all left me a bit breathless but what memories to look back on. All of them!

KENT

First Innings		Second Innings	
M.H. Denness c and b Wilson	42	c Binks b Trueman	2
B.W. Luckhurst not out	1	c Illingworth b Wilson	0
D. Nicholls c Hampshire b Hutton	12	b Nicholson	0
J. Shepherd c Nicholson b Hutton	5	b Nicholson	13
S.E. Leary b Hutton	66	c Trueman b Nicholson	0
R.C. Wilson c Sharpe b Illingworth	19	c and b Hutton	50
A.L. Dixon c Hutton b Illingworth	18	lbw b Illingworth	18
T.G. Evans b Illingworth	10	c Padgett b Hutton	6
G.W. Johnson b Trueman	8	b Illingworth	2
A. Brown b Trueman	33	not out	0
J.N. Graham b Nicholson	3	b Nicholson	1
Extras	6	Extras	8
Total	223	Total	100

YORKSHIRE

First Innings		Second Innings	
P.J. Sharpe c Johnson b Brown	56	c Shepherd b Dixon	37
K. Taylor c Evans b Brown	20	c Denness b Graham	9
D.E.V. Padgett c Leary b Dixon	18	not out	30
J.H. Hampshire c Johnson b Dixon	26	c Brown b Johnson	21
J.C. Balderstone lbw b Dixon	1	not out	1
R. Illingworth c Evans b Dixon	0		
R.A. Hutton b Dixon	8		
J.G. Binks c Shepherd b Graham	14		
D. Wilson b Dixon	37		
F.S. Trueman c sub b Dixon	33		
A.G. Nicholson not out	1		
Extras	11	Extras	1
Total	225	Total (for 3 wkts)	99

Bowling
KENT (first innings): Trueman 10.1-2-39-2; Nicholson 12-2-29-1; Hutton 17-2-65-3; Wilson 23-15-26-1; Illingworth 26-7-58-3. (second innings): Trueman 4-2-3-1; Nicholson 11.3-3-37-4; Hutton 10-4-15-2; Illingworth 14-5-25-2. Wilson 10-4-12-1.
YORKSHIRE (first innings): Graham 37-13-60-0; Brown 18-3-61-2; Dixon 29.2-7-93-7; (second innings): Graham 5-1-20-1; Brown 7-1-12-0; Shepherd 12-4-28-0; Dixon 4-1-31-3; Johnson 5-2-7-1.

20

Fred
Trueman

Yorkshire v Australians
Sheffield 1968
29th June, 1st, 2nd July

FREDERICK SEWARDS TRUEMAN OBE, *born 6.2.1931, Stainton. Right-arm fast bowler, vigorous right-hand batsman. The greatest fast bowler England has ever produced, he took 2,300 wickets in his career and reached 300 Test wickets in his 65th international match. He took 29 wickets in his first Test series with a best return of 8-31. On no fewer than 12 occasions he had 100 or more victims in a season and in 1960 he took 175 wickets at an average of 13.98. He hit over 9,000 first-class runs including three centuries and held 439 catches. Twenty-five years after retiring he travels all over the world to carry out public speaking engagements; he writes books, magazine and newspaper articles and broadcasts regularly on Radio and TV.*

I didn't often get a chance to captain Yorkshire – certainly not as often as I would have liked. That usually had to wait until Brian Close was injured and as he was as tough as old boots, *that* didn't happen very often. But he was out of the side when the Australian tourists came to Bramall Lane in 1968 and so I was able to skipper Yorkshire in what would be my last game against the Aussies – and that was a game I wanted to be able to remember for the rest of my life.

We won the toss and decided to bat but it was a pretty good side that Bill Lawry had and they gave absolutely nothing away in the field. By the end of the first day we had reached 271 for four which was neither here nor there in terms of getting a win out of the game. Next morning Bill said to me, "You've declared, haven't you?" It was more of a statement than a question and I replied, "No. We're batting on." A few minutes later Brian Sellers, the Yorkshire chairman, asked, "What's all this about batting on?" "We haven't got enough runs to declare," I replied. "As things are, the best we can hope for is a draw, and I want to get 50 or 60 more runs and then try to bowl them out twice."

He looked neither convinced nor happy and off he went. We batted solidly down to No.6 and all the top batsmen got runs so we were able to declare at 355 for nine 40 minutes before lunch.

And let me stress that it hadn't been easy. It was hot and steamy so there was help for the swing and seam bowlers; the pitch also was a bit useful to the spinners. The Australian attack consisted of three quick bowlers – McKenzie, Renneberg and Connolly – the leg-spinner Gleeson, Ian Chappell who mixed up leg-spin with little seamers, and Doug Walters who somehow contrived to produce the unexpected. So we'd had to work for our runs; I was determined that the Aussies were going to have to work even harder for theirs.

I was 37 years old and this was my 20th season in first-class cricket, but I used the long run at the start of the Australian first innings. It felt good. In my heart I was a youngster again, playing a big match for the first time. I desperately wanted to beat the Aussies. I had started thinking about retirement but I hadn't said anything about it to anyone. There was a job to be done first.

When he'd made 26, I had Ian Redpath caught by Jimmy Binks and Walters came in at No.3. Dick Hutton found an edge and I took off. I must say I was rather glad to hold on to that one whilst airborne: 36 for two. Then came a storm which had been threatening and we lost time we simply couldn't afford. We started again and now I caught Lawry and Paul Sheahan and ran out Chappell with a throw from cover – don't ask what I was doing there! – which gave me a lot of pleasure. Then Ray Illingworth spun out the middle and I picked up the last two wickets (Gleeson and Connolly). We had forced the Aussies into half-an-hour's batting before lunch; now we had another 20 minutes at them before close of play. The lead was only just over 200 but I certainly wasn't going to let that advantage slip. When their ninth wicket fell at 147 the groundsman came out to ask which roller I wanted for the second innings and nothing had pleased me as much for a long time as being able to signal him to ask Bill Lawry, not me!

And when Hutton bowled Lawry for a duck I knew we could win. "Thanks, Dick," I said, "You've just won the game for us." Lawry could have batted all next day; he was that sort of player. I went to bed with a little prayer for good weather next day.

On the third morning some people seemed to want a Press conference before play had even started. The usual daft question came, sure enough: "What time would we win?" I replied, briskly, "Half-past three," and got on with my preparations. Hutton again took a priceless early wicket but then Walters and Sheahan put on 50 and time was ticking by. I came back for a second spell and removed Sheahan's middle stump. Raymond then took a catch in the gulley to shift Walters and we were back in business. Illy winkled out the middle order again and when the last wicket fell it was exactly half-past three!

Well, I'd better not say more about it except that it was the best moment in my cricketing life. This is what some other people said:

Wisden – "Inflicting their first defeat of the tour on the Australians, Yorkshire gave an impressive display of purposeful cricket. Only in fielding were the tourists, strongly represented, a comparable force, the Yorkshire batting and bowling showing vastly superior adaptation to the playing conditions and a pitch that gave some, but certainly not excessive, help to both fast bowling and slow. It was Yorkshire's first victory against an Australian side since 1902."

Michael Melford, in the *Daily Telegraph* – "Trueman directed

Cartoon by Roy Ullyett.

affairs with good sense and bowled with a pace and stamina which legend said had been lost some way back in an honourable career.

"When people look at the scores in years to come they will conclude that for the Australians to have been bowled out for 148 and 138 the pitch must have broken up. But an occasional eccentric bounce, a gentle receptiveness to spin, varying light and a heavy atmosphere were the limit of the batsman's problems. Yorkshire, and Trueman, did the rest.

"Trueman, aged 37, was standing in as captain in the absence of

Brian Close. He won the toss, batted and declared at 355-9 on the second day. In an inspired personal performance and bowling from his longest run, Trueman took four for 32, held three catches and ran out one Australian. He then enforced the follow-on and with 20 minutes remaining began a venomous spell... Next morning he predicted: 'Yorkshire will win at 3.30pm.' With Ray Illingworth taking four for 23 and Trueman three for 51 his forecast was accurate, to the minute."

And perhaps what pleased me most of all, Len Hutton watched the game, sitting with Bill Bowes. He had had many battles with the Aussies himself, especially as captain. He then wrote to a friend of mine: "Fred was a good captain."

That'll do for me.

As for the team, I was proud of 'em. They played like Yorkshiremen.

But even after all that, there was still another fight to come. The Yorkshire Committee said there would be no £5 win-bonus because it hadn't been a county championship match. Winning the championship was certainly important, very much more so to us than to the Committee! But we all felt that beating the Aussies for the first time in 66 years was a bit special. It was the first time they had been beaten on that tour; it hadn't been a fluke and we hadn't done it against a weak side – eight of them had played against England in the previous Test. And we weren't so well-off that we could turn our noses up at a bonus.

Pay at that time was £22 for an away match and £14 for a home game, out of which we had to pay our own expenses so an extra fiver was always welcome. But the Committee said "No" and I had to have a right set-to with Brian Sellers before the decision was changed.

It wasn't the only spot of bother we had with the Committee, either. Closey had more than one row with them; both Jimmy Binks and Ray Illingworth would have stayed Yorkshire players for longer than they did if there had been a bit more "give" and less "take" from the Committee. There were times when we seemed to be treated more like slaves than championship cricketers and, looking back, it seems amazing that we never let it affect the way we played our cricket. Having bother *off* the field was one thing; getting stuck into the opposition *on* the field was something different altogether. We weren't very good at the first; we were not bad at the other.

At the same time it's important to remember that everyone seemed to play the game that little bit harder against us and some didn't confine their efforts to the period when play was actually taking place. I remember a game in 1963 at Edgbaston... In the previous match I had developed a painful blister on the sole of one foot where the sock had rolled up into a tight little ball. It was obvious that I would have to miss the next game and this news was duly published in the newspapers. By the time we got to Birmingham, George Alcock, our physiotherapist, had eased the pain quite a bit by cutting a piece of sorbo-rubber to fit round the blister and he applied a new sort of medication which had just come onto the market. It felt a lot better.

Closey asked me, "Have you had a look at the pitch" and I said, "Yes. The usual sort of thing at Edgbaston... no grass, flat... bloody awful."

"No," he replied. "We are not using that one. *That's* the pitch for this game... (pointing) a bit further across the square."

I looked out and saw a lovely, lush, green strip. My blister began to feel *a lot* easier. I went out and had another look. It was grassy... covered in a lovely green growth.

I said to George Alcock, "Let's have another dressing on the blister," and to the captain I said, "I'm playing."

Closey went off to exchange teams with Mike Smith who looked a bit surprised when he saw my name. "I thought Trueman wasn't fit?" he inquired.

"He is now he has seen the pitch you have chosen," replied Closey.

We got 261, thanks to a marvellous not out hundred by Ray Illingworth and 78 from Jackie Hampshire. I got four for 14 in the Warwickshire first innings and six for 18 in the second. Mel Ryan took four for 13 and three for 29. Warwickshire were bowled out for 35 (in less than 22 overs) and 55 (29.5 overs) on a pitch they had so obviously (and flatteringly) prepared for my absence and on which they expected to win. After scoring only 261, Yorkshire won by an innings and 171 runs at twenty minutes to five on the second day.

Mike Smith did not bat in the game because of injury and Alan Smith, captain in his absence, murmured, with a wry grin that Monday evening, "And we haven't even saved the follow-on!"

Days like that on the field made up for the way we were treated by the Committee off it. Looking back, I marvel that we tolerated the official attitude towards us because it really was pretty rough. No one, it seemed, ever thought of organising a celebration dinner, or even a lunch, when we won the championship. We never got so much as a tankard to mark those occasions. D'you know, when I passed Brian Statham's record of Test wickets (we were on tour in New Zealand) I received congratulatory telegrams from every county – and even from MCC – except Yorkshire! We were just expected to get on with it and not make a fuss about anything. It's probably best summed up by that famous remark of Arthur Mitchell's to Ellis Robinson in the great Yorkshire team of the 1930s.

Ellis had dived full-length to hold a blinding catch inches from the ground and as the crowd roared its applause Ellis looked up at his

Spectators cram into the Scarborough ground for the 1965 festival. (Photo by Patrick Eagar)

team-mates in the close-catching positions, expecting at least a bit of approval. All he got was a reproof from the grim-faced "Ticker":

"Gerrup and stop makin' an exhibition o' thissen."

No. There wasn't a lot of sentiment around. If we had any sort of celebration get-together it had to be something we had organised ourselves. In fact we wouldn't have thought of fixing up a celebration. That only came when we attended each other's weddings or birthdays.

And yet when we went out to play we were 11 proud Yorkshiremen. I remember once, as we took the field at Lord's, Dusty Rhodes – one of the umpires – remarking, "You *look* like a team." Other teams used to reckon our attitude and our appearance was worth about three wickets start. David Lloyd, later to become Lancashire's captain (and today their coach), tells the story of sitting as a young player in the pavilion before a Roses match and confessing, "We were frightened to death at the very sight of the Yorkshire team. We didn't show it, of course. But just looking at them made us shiver a bit."

And we *were* a great side – no doubt about it. There was Tony Nicholson and Dick Hutton to share the quick bowling with me; Raymond, a great thinking bowler; Closey, who was always *doing* something, either with the ball or moving the field around. And Wils (Don Wilson), not the greatest slow left-armer Yorkshire had ever had but what an enthusiast! He never stopped trying and when things were going well he was just like a little lad. I remember the first time he took Peter May's wicket he started racing about and waving his arms till I shouted to Closey, "For God's sake shut t'gate or he'll run all the way to Settle to tell 'em what he's done."

In 1967 at Middlesbrough he took seven for 21 against Warwickshire after I had bowled a bit quick at the start of the day (*Fred's opening spell, in fact read 5-5-0-3 – DM*) and his delight was wonderful to see. And he was a great man in the field as well as hitting the ball many a mile with his left-handed batting. At Sheffield, in 1960, he hit 83 out of our total of 196 against Surrey and that involved batting against Alec Bedser and Peter Loader, not the easiest bowlers to knock around.

Yes, we were a pretty good side in the 1960s. I had my share of arguments. I had one or two right up-and-downers with Closey and I didn't get on all that well with Vic Wilson. But once we stepped out onto the field, no matter where it was, we were a *team* and we were representing Yorkshire. That was enough.

In 20 years, I played in a lot of sides, under a lot of captains, in a lot of countries. Those lads of the 1960s still share a lot of good memories with me.

YORKSHIRE

First Innings

G. Boycott c Taber b Chappell	86
P.J. Sharpe c Lawry b Gleeson	47
D.E.V. Padgett c Taber b Gleeson	56
J.H. Hampshire c Lawry b Gleeson	33
K. Taylor c Taber b McKenzie	24
R. Illingworth not out	69
J.G. Binks c Taber b McKenzie	0
R.A. Hutton c Walters b McKenzie	2
F.S. Trueman c Sheahan b Gleeson	13
D. Wilson c Redpath b McKenzie	0
P.M. Stringer not out	12
Extras	13
Total (for 9 wkts dec)	355

AUSTRALIANS

First Innings		Second Innings	
W.M. Lawry c Trueman b Illingworth	58	b Hutton	0
I.R. Redpath c Binks b Trueman	12	lbw b Hutton	12
K.D. Walters c Trueman b Hutton	4	c Illingworth b Trueman	62
A.P. Sheahan c Trueman b Hutton	10	b Trueman	17
I.M. Chappell run out	18	c Hutton b Illingworth	26
R.J. Inverarity c Stringer b Illingworth	2	lbw b Illingworth	1
H.E. Taber b Illingworth	9	st Binks b Illingworth	0
G.D. McKenzie c Hutton b Illingworth	6	c Binks b Trueman	0
J.W. Gleeson b Trueman	4	b Illingworth	12
A.N. Connolly b Trueman	20	run out	0
D.A. Renneberg not out	0	not out	4
Extras	5	Extras	4
Total	148	Total	138

Bowling

YORKSHIRE: McKenzie 27-7-73-4; Renneberg 19-2-58-0; Connolly 32-16-49-0; Gleeson 47-12-123-4; Chappell 6-0-33-1; Walters 7-5-6-0.
AUSTRALIANS (first innings): Trueman 10.2-2-32-3; Hutton 12-3-37-2; Stringer 4-2-6-0; Illingworth 17-3-44-4; Wilson 9-1-20-0; Taylor 1-0-4-0.
(second innings): Trueman 19-4-51-3; Hutton 12-5-35-2; Illingworth 22-12-23-4; Wilson 13.1-7-25-0; Boycott 1-1-0-0.

21

Tony Nicholson

Kent v Yorkshire
Canterbury 1968
31st July, 1st, 2nd August

A NTHONY GEORGE NICHOLSON, *born 25.6.1938,*
Dewsbury. Died 3.11.1985. Right-arm medium-paced bowler,
right-hand bat. Played 282 matches for Yorkshire between
1962 and 1975, taking 876 wickets for the county. He was, in the
words of Freddie Trueman, the best bowler never to play for England.
Would probably have done so in the winter of 1964-65 when he was
selected for the MCC tour of South Africa but was prevented by
injury from making the trip.

"Nick", as he was affectionately known to his team-mates and, indeed, throughout cricket, is the only regular player of the 1960s who could not be invited to contribute a favourite memory because of his death when he was 47 years old. The huge turnout for his funeral service has been likened to that for an earlier Yorkshire player, Roy Kilner, in 1928.

It is a fact that both men enjoyed the affection and respect of their fellows wherever the game was played.

Nick made his first appearance in 1962 and, with the help of a fairly substantial not-out knock in Essex, he ended with a batting average of 49 for the season. His sense of humour was such that, given the choice, he would probably have opted for that batting performance as his favourite memory. It is doubtful whether he would have chosen an outstanding bowling performance, such as his nine for 62 against Sussex at Eastbourne in 1967, his Roses match 7-32 in 1964, or his 12 for 73 in a match (6-29 and 6-44) against Glamorgan at Headingley in 1964. So we asked his widow, Ann (another great Yorkshire cricket enthusiast) to suggest one.

And she replied, "I suppose one of his best memories would be of Canterbury in 1968."

In fact it was in some ways a great day... for Kent. There were 12,000 people in the ground when the game began and the teams were introduced to the Duke of Kent, as Patron of Kent CCC. But HRH was accompanied by his Duchess, the former Miss Katherine Worsley, of Hovingham Hall, who just happened to be Patron of Yorkshire CCC! And Nick was one of those introduced to her.

The conditions were made for swing bowlers and Nick took full advantage. He bowled a formidable outswinger which, at first glance, seemed remarkable in itself because he had a pronounced chest-on delivery from which one would have expected the opposite kind of deviation. But he achieved the out-swing by the positioning of his feet at the moment of delivery and the ensuing body-movement. On Wednesday, 31st July, 1968, Nick found himself able to move the ball late enough to induce strokes but controlled his pace so admirably

Peter Parfitt scrapes home with Jimmy Binks at the wicket during the MCC v Yorkshire match at Lord's in 1962. (Photo by S&G Press Agency)

that Jimmy Binks actually produced two stumpings off his bowling. His senior partner, FST, took the second and eighth wickets, Nick grabbed the remainder: 12-4-22-8.

The sun never broke through but it was a day of high summer so the atmosphere was warm and oppressive, the sort of day a swing bowler dreams about. It is probably fair to say that Her Royal Highness got a good deal of pleasure out of seeing her native county dispose of the opposition for 81. And then it rained all day Thursday!

Both sides, contenders for the county championship, made strenuous efforts to achieve a result. Yorkshire scraped a first innings lead despite all the efforts of the left-arm seamer John Dye and the West Indian all-rounder John Shepherd. And in fact Nick played his part (in a ninth-wicket partnership with Richard Hutton) in preventing Kent from getting the fifth bonus point. After three-quarters-of-an-hour on Friday morning, Close declared in the hope of another quick dismissal of Kent. This was not to be. Nick, however, clean bowled an England captain (Mike Denness) and a Pakistan skipper (Asif Iqbal) as Kent reached a formal declaration-point at 136 for five, and there was time for only three further overs in the game. That was enough to give Nick ten wickets in the match.

In his 20 seasons with Yorkshire, Freddie Trueman had more than 40 opening partners and he rated Tony Nicholson the best of them. He was a great-hearted bowler with an engaging character who absolutely loved his playing days with Yorkshire. He would have similarly enjoyed sharing with us his outstanding memories of the heady days of the 1960s.

KENT

First Innings		Second Innings	
M.H. Denness c Sharpe b Nicholson	18	b Nicholson	15
B.W. Luckhurst c Close b Nicholson	2	c Illingworth b Close	42
G.W. Johnson c Binks b Trueman	2	not out	7
Asif Iqbal lbw b Nicholson	30	b Nicholson	1
S.E. Leary st Binks b Nicholson	4	c Taylor b Wilson	13
J.N. Shepherd b Nicholson	3	not out	18
A.P.E. Knott st Binks b Nicholson	1	c Hampshire b Wilson	29
D.L. Underwood lbw b Nicholson	10		
A.L. Dixon b Trueman	3		
D.M. Sayer not out	3		
D.C. Dye lbw b Nicholson	1		
Extras	4	Extras	11
Total	81	Total (for 5 wkts dec)	136

YORKSHIRE

First Innings		Second Innings	
P.J. Sharpe lbw b Dye	11	not out	2
K. Taylor c Knott b Dye	1	not out	0
D.E.V. Padgett c Knott b Dye	7		
J.H. Hampshire lbw b Shepherd	28		
D.B. Close c Knott b Shepherd	1		
R. Illingworth c Luckhurst b Sayer	0		
J.G. Binks b Shepherd	3		
R.A. Hutton not out	31		
F.S. Trueman b Shepherd	0		
D. Wilson lbw b Dye	6		
A.G. Nicholson not out	3		
Extras	2		
Total (for 9 wkts dec)	93	Total (for no wkt)	2

Bowling
KENT (first innings): Trueman 8-1-25-2; Nicholson 12-4-22-8; Hutton 7-1-30-0; (second innings): Trueman 7-2-18-0; Nicholson 17-9-33-2; Hutton 14-3-36-0; Illingworth 2-0-10-0; Wilson 8-3-21-2; Close 3-0-7-1.
YORKSHIRE (first innings): Dye 22-9-42-4; Sayer 6-1-10-1; Shepherd 23-16-29-4; Dixon 3-1-10-0; Underwood 1-1-0-0; (second innings): Shepherd 2-1-2-0; Underwood 1-1-0-0.

22

Brian
Close

Yorkshire v Surrey
Anlaby Road, Hull 1968
28th, 29th, 30th August

DENNIS BRIAN CLOSE CBE, *born 24.2.1931, Rawdon. Left-hand bat, right-arm medium-fast or off-spin bowler, brilliant closefield. A precociously-talented teenager, Close played the first of his 536 matches for Yorkshire in 1949, a season in which he completed the double of 1,000 runs and 100 wickets and was selected by England before he had been awarded his Yorkshire cap. After being sensationally and controversially sacked by Yorkshire he spent 1971 to 1977 with Somerset where he saw the blossoming careers of Vivian Richards and Ian Botham as well as sowing the seeds of the county's subsequent successes. A great tactician with splendid flair, he led Yorkshire to the county championship title in 1963, 1966, 1967, and 1968 and they won the Gillette Cup in 1965 and 1969. Captain of England in 1966 and 1967, Close never lost a Test. Football for Arsenal, Leeds United and Bradford City; he is or has been a gifted golfer, tennis and snooker player. In the last decade he has been a member of the Yorkshire CCC Committee, notably as Chairman of Cricket.*

Editor's note: Before we look at Close's selected match it is as well to check his record of indestructibility. Against Gloucs, he was famously hit on the forehead by a shot from Martin Young who then saw the ball rebound to give a catch to Philip Sharpe, in the slips. Again against Gloucs, this time at Harrogate, he took a square cut from Ron Nicholls on the forehead but resumed his fielding position at once, ignoring the blood pouring down his face and soaking his shirt. George Alcock, the physiotherapist, ran onto the field and insisted on treating the cut despite Close's protestations. At Portsmouth, Richard Gilliat, of Hampshire, hit a ball into Close's face and it rebounded so far over a slow and rain-soaked outfield that the batsmen ran three. In the 1963 Test v West Indies at Lord's, Close scored 70 (out of England's second-innings total of 228-9) by advancing down the pitch to the bowling of Wes Hall and Charlie Griffith and taking short-pitched deliveries on his body. ("Well, I couldn't be out lbw and they weren't going to bowl me.") The following day the whole right side of his body was a mass of blue-and-purple bruises. Recalled to the Test side at the age of 45, he opened England's innings against West Indies at Old Trafford in 1976 and took another battering from Andy Roberts, Michael Holding and Wayne Daniel in which his "box" was smashed and splintered. He batted on – with the most delicate part of his anatomy impaled on the splintered plastic . . .

This was our last championship game of the season and we were in close contention with Kent. Glamorgan weren't out of it, either. They had beaten us at Sheffield five weeks earlier when we were asked to get 205 in the fourth innings at 80 an hour. No one ever set us an easy target and we were lucky if we got a reasonable one but we didn't moan about that. It was what we expected. What we couldn't cope with was the weather which resulted in three drawn games towards the end of July and the beginning of August. We beat Somerset at Scarborough and saw most of the match against Derbyshire at Park Avenue washed away. Then we lost at Worcester *by one run* in a very low-scoring game in which the last pair, Trueman and Nicholson, came together with 16 runs needed. They got 14 of them before Fred, who had survived four lbw appeals, was given out to the fifth. A draw at Chesterfield in the penultimate fixture meant that everything depended on the last one.

We lost the toss, were put in to bat and scoring was never easy so that we reached 221 for eight with about an hour-and-a-half remaining. At that point, Ray Illingworth and Don Wilson suddenly cut loose and added 85 in 70 minutes. We declared at 327 for nine, got a lead of 138, mucked the batting order about a bit and were finally able to set Surrey 250 to win at around 55 an hour with just about enough time to bowl them out. They started well enough with Mike Edwards and Roger Knight making 56 before we took a wicket. Then Ray and Don did their stuff again, this time with the ball, and Surrey were struggling at 84 for six. This brought together Younis Ahmed and Arnold Long, the wicket-keeper. Younis was a dashing sort of batsman, always looking to play a few shots, while Arnold clung on grimly in support. It created a few problems with field-placing, that, because we had to keep one eye on the clock as well as trying to take wickets. It was a 4.30 or 5pm finish but there was never any question that we would take the extra half-hour. We had got to win it.

Younis and Long took the score to 121 and then Younis swept at Wils. It was firmly struck and the ball hit me full on the shin and ricochetted away, hitting Jackie Hampshire somewhere round the ankle. He started hopping around and I snarled at him: "Get the ball back to Wils and let's get on." Glowering, Hamps tossed the ball back to the bowler but there was now another delay. Wilson, white-faced and eyes bulging, was now pointing to my leg (blood was staining my flannels and running down into my boot). He gulped:

"You'll have to go off, Skipper, and get that seen to."

"Get on with it," I bawled back at him.

Younis, meanwhile, was looking a bit displeased. He'd hoped to get four for his shot and he'd got none. I moved half-a-yard closer at short leg. So when Wils finally got round to bowling the next ball

Ray Illingworth cuts Barber to slip fielder A.R. Lewis during the MCC v Yorkshire match at Lord's in 1964 (Photo by S&G Press Agency)

Younis tried another sweep. I braced myself, as you do when you know a blow is coming, with my arms tight to my sides... trying to make a smaller target, I suppose. The ball hit me somewhere on the side of my body and the inside of my arm and this time it rebounded in the air instead of close to the ground. Jimmy Binks took the catch. Poor Younis, who again had been expecting a four, obviously couldn't believe what was happening. He just stood there. We had to appeal to

the umpire, Albert Gaskell, who said, "Batsman – you're out." So off
he went. Younis had scored 75.

I've completely forgotten how we came to run out Pat Pocock but
Robin Jackman came in, on a pair, played back instead of forward to
Wilson and found it was the arm-ball: lbw, 0. He'd bagged 'em. I
brought back Nick (Tony Nicholson) and with Jimmy Binks standing
up to the stumps he caught Long for 22. We had won by 60 runs – the
game and the county championship. There were just five minutes play
left in the match.

Wisden prosaically records: "Yorkshire forced victory by taking the
last three wickets in two overs after having been held back by Younis
Ahmed and Long for an hour-and-threequarters." It wasn't quite as
straightforward as that. They had both played bloody well and we
had tried every change and combination of our six bowlers but
nothing seemed to work. I was reduced to trying to dream up what
came next when Younis tried the sweep – twice.

The leg? Oh, that was a damn nuisance. The champagne was
flowing and a bit of a party was starting when the doctor came in and
ordered me to go to hospital for an anti-tetanus injection. You know
what hospitals are like. I missed all the champagne and most of
the party.

[That was the last time Yorkshire won the county championship.]

YORKSHIRE

First Innings		Second Innings	
P.J. Sharpe c Stewart b Jackman	9	c Jackman b Pocock	18
K. Taylor c Barrington b Selvey	16	c Stewart b Jackman	16
D.E.V. Padgett lbw b Pocock	65	c Roope b Jackman	20
J.H. Hampshire c Long b Jackman	3	c Hooper b Jackman	9
D.B. Close c Hooper b Jackman	72	not out	3
R. Illingworth c and b Jackman	66	not out	25
J.G. Binks c Roope b Knight	3	c Long b Jackman	8
R.A. Hutton b Selvey	3	Did not bat	
F.S. Trueman c Long b Jackman	0	c Edwards b Jackman	5
D. Wilson not out	61	b Jackman	3
A.G. Nicholson not out	9	Did not bat	
Extras	20	Extras	5
Total (9 wkts.)	*327	Total (7 wkts.)	*112

*Innings declared closed

SURREY

First Innings		Second Innings	
M.J. Edwards c Hampshire b Nicholson	28	c Hampshire b Illingworth	29
R.D.V. Knight c Hampshire b Wilson	64	b Wilson	36
M.J. Stewart lbw b Nicholson	0	lbw b Illingworth	0
K.F. Barrington c Hutton b Illingworth	10	c Nicholson b Wilson	9
Younis Ahmed c Hampshire b Illingworth	1	c Binks b Wilson	75
G.R.G. Roope lbw b Wilson	36	lbw b Illingworth	0
J.M. Hooper c Sharpe b Wilson	8	b Wilson	4
A. Long lbw b Close	9	c Binks b Nicholson	22
P.I. Pocock not out	25	run out	10
R.D. Jackman b Wilson	0	lbw b Wilson	0
M.W.W. Selvey c Hampshire b Illingworth	1	not out	0
Extras	7	Extras	5
Total	189	Total	190

Bowling
YORKSHIRE (first innings): Jackman 31-7-65-5; Selvey 29-5-94-2; Roope 20-2-67-0; Pocock 17-5-42-1; Knight 16-3-39-1; (second innings): Jackman 19-0-58-6; Selvey 5-1-14-0; Pocock 14-1-35-1.
SURREY (first innings): Trueman 6-1-11-0; Nicholson 16-6-29-2; Close 3-0-15-1; Hutton 3-1-4-0; Wilson 30-8-48-4; Illingworth 32.2-9-75-3; (second innings): Trueman 6-1-13-0; Nicholson 13-3-34-1; Hutton 3-0-11-0; Illingworth 28-12-49-3; Wilson 24-4-61-5; Close 6-2-17-0.

23

Yorkshire
County Cricket Club

First team
batting and bowling averages
and final
County Championship
positions

1959-1968

1959
County Championship

BATTING AVERAGES

Batsman	No. of Innings	Times Not Out	Highest Score	Total Runs	Average
R. Illingworth	36	10	150	1105	42·50
D.E.V. Padgett	50	7	139	1807	42·03
H.D. Bird	10	2	181*	316	39·50
J.B. Bolus	14	5	91	340	38·33
W.B. Stott	47	2	144*	1694	37·64
D.B. Close	46	1	154	1317	29·26
K. Taylor	42	1	144	1126	27·46
P.J. Sharpe	25	1	73	608	25·33
J.V. Wilson	25	4	105	505	24·02
F.S. Trueman	28	5	54	433	18·82
J. Birkenshaw	13	2	38	164	13·66
D. Wilson	31	5	65	351	11·32
J.R. Burnet	36	1	47	383	10·94
J.G. Binks	35	6	37	305	10·52
R.K. Platt	29	13	57	130	8·12

The following also batted:
M. Ryan 4*, 12*, 5*, 17;
D. Pickles 0*, 1*, 0;
C.H. Wood 4, 8, 10;
B. Stead 8, 0.

*Signifies not out.

1959
County Championship

BOWLING AVERAGES

Bowler	Overs	Maidens	Runs	Wickets	Average
F.S. Trueman	716·3	177	1791	93	19·26
R.K Platt	844·2	266	1872	85	22·24
M. Ryan	177·4	44	471	21	22·43
R. Illingworth	724·3	238	1663	82	22·81
K. Taylor	218	68	484	20	24·20
D.B. Close	684·4	197	1893	75	25·24
C.H. Wood	91·4	17	263	10	26·30
D. Wilson	601·2	184	1559	53	29·41
J. Birkenshaw	252	73	645	19	33·95
D. Pickles	111	19	374	6	62·33
The following also bowled:					
W.B. Stott	6	2	17	1	
D.E.V. Padgett	17·1	6	46	–	
J.V. Wilson	7	1	24	–	
J.R. Burnet	2	–	21	1	
P.J. Sharpe	1	1	–	–	
J.B. Bolus	6	1	19	–	
B. Stead	15	1	39	–	

1959
County Championship

FINAL POSITIONS

	P	W	L	D	No dec.	1st inns. lead in match L	1st inns. lead in match D	Bns pts.	Pts.
Points awarded	–	12	–	–	–	2	2	–	–
Yorkshire	28	14	7	7	0	0	5	26	204
Gloucestershire	28	12	11	5*	0	1	3	28	186
Surrey	28	12	5	11	0	0	8	26	186
Warwickshire	28	13	10	5	0	2	1	22	184
Lancashire	28	12	7	9	0	1	5	28	184
Glamorgan	28	12	8	7	1	3	4	20	178
Derbyshire	28	12	6	10	0	3	2	20	174
Hampshire	28	11	10	7	0	1	4	26	168
Essex	28	11	7	10*	0	0	4	22	168
Middlesex	28	10	9	9	0	3	3	24	157
Northamptonshire	28	8	10	10	0	4	9	24	146
Somerset	28	8	13	.7	0	4	3	20	130
Kent	28	8	12	8	0	2	5	18	128
Worcestershire	28	6	8	13	1	1	7	18	106
Sussex	28	6	11	10	1	3	3	18	102
Leicestershire	28	5	16	7	0	0	2	8	72
Nottinghamshire	28	4	14	9	1	1	3	6	62

*Including a Tie

1960
County Championship

BATTING AVERAGES

Batsman	No. of Innings	Times Not Out	Highest Score	Total Runs	Average
D.E.V. Padgett	36	2	146	1420	41·75
D.B. Close	46	3	198	1650	38·40
W.B. Stott	46	4	186	1548	36·80
K. Taylor	37	5	130*	994	31·20
R. Illingworth	30	6	86	661	27·54
J.B. Bolus	38	5	146*	885	26·81
J.V. Wilson	40	7	84*	855	25·92
P.J. Sharpe	28	3	152	635	25·40
F.S. Trueman	26	4	69	455	20·68
J. Birkenshaw	18	4	42	248	18·00
D. Wilson	39	3	83	511	14·19
J.G. Binks	36	11	23	305	12·20
R.K. Platt	6	1	23*	42	8·40
M. Ryan	13	3	15	44	4·40
M.J. Cowan	26	10	7	36	2·25

The following also batted:
J.P.G. Chadwick 10, 4, 6;
A.G. Hatton 4*;
D. Pickles 7*.

*Signifies not out.

1960
County Championship

BOWLING AVERAGES

Bowler	Overs	Maidens	Runs	Wickets	Average
F.S. Trueman	795·5	217	1687	132	12·79
R. Illingworth	716·3	309	1350	75	18·88
M. Ryan	360·5	99	834	37	22·54
R.K. Platt	265.2	78	578	24	24·01
D. Wilson	906·1	412	1597	72	22·18
M.J. Cowan	701·4	175	1505	66	22·81
D.B. Close	575·3	186	1434	63	22·79
J. Birkenshaw	208	65	621	26	23·88
K. Taylor	138	47	289	9	32·10
The following also bowled:					
A.G. Hatton	45	9	136	6	
J.V. Wilson	0·5	–	1	–	
J.B. Bolus	14.2	6	28	–	
D. Pickles	22.4	10	21	4	
B. Turner	20	12	17	3	

1960
County Championship

FINAL POSITIONS

	P	W	L	D	No dec.	1st inns. lead in match L	1st inns. lead in match D	Bns pts.	Pts.
Points awarded	–	12	–	–	–	2	2	–	–
Yorkshire	32	17	6	6	3	2	2	34	246
Lancashire	32	13	8	10	1	3	9	34	214
Middlesex	28	12	4	12	0	0	7	28	186
Sussex	32	12	6	12	2	2	6	28	188
Derbyshire	28	10	7	10	1	1	5	20	152
Essex	28	9	3	14	2	1	7	28	152
Surrey	28	9	6	10	3	2	3	20	138
Gloucestershire	28	9	7	12	0	0	3	16	130
Northamptonshire	28	8	6	13	1	1	6	16	126
Kent	28	7	7	12	2	1	6	20	118
Glamorgan	32	9	14	7	2	0	4	16	133
Hampshire	32	8	8	14	2	1	6	22	132
Worcestershire	32	8	12	10	2	1	6	20	130
Somerset	32	5	11	15	1	2	10	22	106
Warwickshire	32	4	12	16	0	2	9	26	96
Nottingham	28	4	16	7	1	4	2	12	72
Leicestershire	28	2	13	12	1	0	5	12	46

The Glamorgan record includes one point for tie on first innings in match lost.

1961
County Championship

BATTING AVERAGES

Batsman	No. of Innings	Times Not Out	Highest Score	Total Runs	Average
J.B. Bolus	48	4	133	1596	36·27
K. Taylor	44	3	203*	1409	34·36
D.B. Close	47	5	132	1405	33·45
D.E.V. Padgett	54	6	114	1532	31·91
W.B. Stott	44	3	116	1174	28·63
P.J. Sharpe	43	6	87	1000	27·02
R. Illingworth	38	4	75	753	22·14
J.V. Wilson	44	8	87	764	21·22
F.S. Trueman	30	3	58	569	21·07
D. Wilson	9	2	31	136	19·42
K. Gillhouley	29	7	56*	306	13·90
J.G. Binks	45	12	58	454	13·75
A.B. Bainbridge	8	0	24	71	8·87
P.J. Kippax	5	2	9	26	8·66
M. Ryan	14	7	17*	45	6·42
R.K. Platt	20	11	12*	54	6·00

The following also batted:
J.H. Hampshire 11 and 61;
J.C. Balderstone 23;
M.J. Cowan 2*, 0*, and 0;
B. Turner 3* and 3*;
A.G. Hatton played in one match but did not bat.   *Signifies not out.

1961
County Championship

BOWLING AVERAGES

Bowler	Overs	Maidens	Runs	Wickets	Average
A.B. Bainbridge	169·4	79	288	19	15·15
R. Illingworth	841·5	357	1618	101	16·01
F.S. Trueman	754·3	220	1781	109	16·33
M.J. Cowan	97·5	25	269	14	19·21
D.B. Close	436·2	177	1036	52	19·92
K. Gillhouley	727	271	1569	73	21·49
R.K. Platt	462	152	1036	48	21·58
M. Ryan	569·5	144	1350	61	22·13
K. Taylor	357	141	690	26	26·53
D. Wilson	173	91	298	11	27·09
J.B. Bolus	46	14	94	3	31·33
P.J. Kippax	84	26	231	7	33·00
The following also bowled:					
W.B. Stott	2·3	0	19	1	
B. Turner	14	6	30	1	
J.V. Wilson	9	0	55	0	
P.J. Sharpe	1	0	1	0	
J.H. Hampshire	1	0	2	0	
J.G. Binks	2	0	11	0	
D.E.V. Padgett	5	1	17	0	
A.G. Hatton	24	3	66	0	

1961
County Championship

FINAL POSITIONS

	P	W	L	D	No dec.	1st inns. lead in match L	1st inns. lead in match D	Bns pts.	Pts.
Points awarded	—	12	—	—	—	2	2	—	—
Hampshire	32	19	7	6	0	1	3	32	268
Yorkshire	32	17	5	10	0	1	5	34	250
Middlesex	28	15	6	6	1	3	1	26	214
Worcestershire	32	16	9	7	0	2	3	24	226
Gloucestershire	28	11	11	5	1	2	2	18	158
Essex	28	10	8	10	0	2	4	26	158
Derbyshire	28	10	9	9	0	3	3	22	154
Sussex	32	11	10	11	0	1	8	20	170
Leicestershire	28	9	13	5	1	2	4	26	146
Somerset	32	10	15	7	0	6	3	24	162
Kent	28	8	8	12	0	1	7	20	132
Warwickshire	32	9	10	13	0	1	7	26	150
Lancashire	32	9	7	15	1	1	7	18	142
Glamorgan	32	9	12	11	0	1	4	10	128
Surrey	28	4	13	11	0	6	8	24	100
Northamptonshire	28	5	13	10	0	1	5	10	82
Nottinghamshire	28	4	20	4	0	6	2	12	76

1962
County Championship

BATTING AVERAGES

Batsman	No. of Innings	Times Not Out	Highest Score	Total Runs	Average
P.J. Sharpe	54	5	138	1872	38·20
D.B. Close	41	5	142*	1356	37·66
R. Illingworth	48	7	127	1468	35·80
D.E.V. Padgett	50	2	125*	1404	29·25
G. Boycott	7	2	47	142	28·40
K. Taylor	36	0	163	986	27·38
J.V. Wilson	48	2	134	1135	24·67
W.B. Stott	28	3	145	609	24·36
J.H. Hampshire	21	2	81	439	23·10
J.B. Bolus	28	0	64	617	22·03
F.S Trueman	32	3	44	583	20·10
R.A. Hutton	9	2	45*	113	16·14
D. Wilson	45	8	41	509	13·75
J.G. Binks	40	7	67	405	12·27
R.K. Platt	12	6	17	63	10·50
M. Ryan	19	7	15*	74	6·16

The following also batted:
A.G. Nicholson 29*, 1;* 2, 0*, 20*, 0, 2, and 37*;
M.J. Cowan 0*, 15*, 0*, 6, 1, 1*, 0*, 4 and 0*;
M.C. Fearnley 11*.   *Signifies not out.

1962
County Championship

BOWLING AVERAGES

Bowler	Overs	Maidens	Runs	Wickets	Average
F.S. Trueman	802	194	1889	106	17·82
R. Illingworth	914	363	1871	102	18·34
R.A. Hutton	56	15	116	6	19·33
M. Ryan	627·1	151	1607	74	21·71
D. Wilson	873	330	1847	83	22·25
R.K. Platt	336·3	108	779	35	22·25
A.G. Nicholson	138	36	406	15	27·06
K. Taylor	330	129	691	25	27·64
D.B. Close	364·5	144	810	28	28·92
M.J. Cowan	255·5	45	722	16	45·12
The following also bowled:					
W.B. Stott	15	6	58	4	
M.C. Fearnley	35·5	13	71	3	
J.B. Bolus	46·3	16	111	2	
J.H. Hampshire	32	7	113	1	
D.E.V. Padgett	21·1	10	32	0	
P.J. Sharpe	10	1	37	0	
J.G. Binks	3	1	15	0	

1962
County Championship

FINAL POSITIONS

	P	W	L	D	No dec.	1st inns. lead in match L	1st inns. lead in match D	Bns pts.	Pts.
Points awarded	–	12	–	–	–	2	2	–	–
Yorkshire	32	14	4	14	0	1	9	36	224
Worcestershire	32	14	3	14	1	1	8	34	220
Warwickshire	32	12	5	15	0	2	11	32	202
Gloucestershire	28	11	11	6	0	5	4	24	174
Surrey	28	10	3	14	1	2	9	32	174
Somerset	32	12	7	13	0	1	7	30	190
Derbyshire	28	8	6	13	1	2	8	28	144
Northamptonshire	28	7	5	16	0	1	10	22	128
Essex	28	8	6	13	1	2	7	12	126
Hampshire	32	7	5	19	1	2	11	30	140
Kent	28	7	9	10	2	2	3	16	110
Sussex	32	7	12	13	0	4	6	18	122
Middlesex	28	6	8	13	1	2	4	18	102
Glamorgan	32	6	13	13	0	1	4	14	96
Nottinghamshire	28	4	12	11	1	0	1	4	54
Lancashire	32	2	16	14	0	6	5	14	60
Leicestershire	28	2	12	13	1	2	5	12	50

1963
County Championship

BATTING AVERAGES

Batsman	No. of Innings	Times Not Out	Highest Score	Total Runs	Average
G. Boycott	38	7	165*	1446	46·64
D.B. Close	28	2	161	915	35·19
K. Taylor	13	2	85	364	33·09
R. Illingworth	22	5	107*	508	29·88
P.J. Sharpe	33	5	138*	766	27·35
W.B. Stott	26	2	143	655	27·29
J. Hampshire	42	4	120	995	26·18
D.E.V. Padgett	33	1	142	811	25·34
F.S. Trueman	21	2	104	356	18·73
R.A. Hutton	11	0	49	191	17·36
A. Clarkson	6	1	30	72	14·40
J.G. Binks	34	6	46*	389	13·89
J.C. Balderstone	10	1	44*	125	13·88
D. Wilson	35	5	44	405	13·50
A.G. Nicholson	19	9	24*	108	10·80
M. Ryan	28	8	26*	207	10·35

The following also batted:
J. Waring 1, 0, 1*, 1 and 17*;
A.B. Bainbridge 12 and 10;
J.P.G. Chadwick 14*;
M.C. Fearnley 0*;
R.K. Platt 0.

*Signifies not out.

1963
County Championship

BOWLING AVERAGES

Bowler	Overs	Maidens	Runs	Wickets	Average
F.S. Trueman	472·2	125	976	76	12·84
J. Waring	72·3	20	196	13	15·07
A.G. Nicholson	527·1	162	1056	65	16·24
R. Illingworth	402·5	157	786	48	16·37
A Clarkson	38	17	92	5	18·40
J. Hampshire	27	2	132	7	18·85
D. Wilson	714·1	275	1552	82	18·92
R.A. Hutton	63·1	13	173	8	21·62
D.B. Close	301·2	107	726	32	22·68
M. Ryan	604·2	163	1309	57	22·96
The following also bowled:					
K. Taylor	67	24	103	4	
J.C. Balderstone	42·4	8	123	3	
J.P.G. Chadwick	21	6	58	2	
D.E.V. Padgett	0·5	0	4	1	
M.C. Fearnley	20	6	37	1	
R.K. Platt	27	9	58	1	
A.B. Bainbridge	31	13	70	1	
P.J. Sharpe	5	1	17	0	
G. Boycott	2	0	20	0	

1963
County Championship

FINAL POSITIONS

	P	W	L	D	No dec.	1st inns. lead in match L	1st inns. lead in match D	Pts.
Points awarded	–	12	–	–	–	2	2	–
Yorkshire	28	13	3	11	1	1	6	144
Glamorgan	28	11	8	8	1	1	6	124
Somerset	28	10	6	11	1	2	7	118
Sussex	28	10	6	12	0	1	7	116
Warwickshire	28	10	3	14	1	1	7	116
Middlesex	28	9	5	11	3	1	7	106
Northamptonshire	28	9	8	11	0	1	5	105
Gloucestershire	28	9	7	11	1	2	3	100
Nottinghamshire	28	6	8	13	1	4	7	82
Hampshire	28	7	8	10	3	1	4	80
Surrey	28	5	6	17	0	1	11	74
Essex	28	6	4	17	1	0	5	70
Kent	28	5	6	17	0	1	8	68
Worcestershire	28	4	8	13	3	2	8	60
Lancashire	28	4	10	13	1	2	7	58
Leicestershire	28	3	13	10	2	2	3	40
Derbyshire	28	2	14	9	3	1	3	28

Northamptonshire gained five points instead of two in drawn match when scores finished level and they were batting.

1964
County Championship

BATTING AVERAGES

Batsman	No. of Innings	Times Not Out	Highest Score	Total Runs	Average
G. Boycott	28	4	177	1427	59·45
R. Illingworth	36	7	135	1055	36·37
K. Taylor	24	2	153	788	35·81
P.J. Sharpe	40	7	79*	1168	35·39
J.G. Binks	32	9	95	729	31·69
D.B. Close	41	6	100*	1077	30·77
D.E.V. Padgett	42	2	112	1144	28·60
J.H. Hampshire	40	4	150	977	27·13
F.S. Trueman	24	3	77	463	22·04
R.A. Hutton	12	1	64	218	19·81
J.C. Balderstone	13	1	58	233	19·41
D. Wilson	33	4	46	485	16·72
B. Wood	7	2	35	63	12·60
M. Ryan	19	9	15*	78	7·80
A.G. Nicholson	14	5	25	61	6·77

The following also batted:
M.C. Fearnley 0 and 8;
J.S. Waring 3 and 1;
G.R. Bloom 2.

*Signifies not out.

1964
County Championship

BOWLING AVERAGES

Bowler	Overs	Maidens	Runs	Wickets	Average
A.G. Nicholson	503·4	145	976	70	13·94
J.C. Balderstone	74·1	36	154	10	15·40
R. Illingworth	867·5	327	1798	104	17·28
F.S. Trueman	556·2	122	1344	67	20·05
M. Ryan	349·4	90	812	39	20·82
R.A Hutton	121·2	33	336	16	21·00
D. Wilson	777·4	306	1542	70	22·02
D.B. Close	460·5	170	1066	47	22·68
The following also bowled:					
M.C. Fearnley	12·5	2	25	2	
D.E.V. Padgett	11	5	27	1	
J.H. Hampshire	29	5	81	1	
K. Taylor	47	9	98	1	
J.S. Waring	16	4	36	0	
G. Boycott	16	4	52	0	
P.J. Sharpe	3	0	17	0	
J.G. Binks	1	0	12	0	

1964
County Championship

FINAL POSITIONS

	P	W	L	D	No dec.	1st inns. lead in match L	1st inns. lead in match D	Pts.
Points awarded	–	12	–	–	–	2	2	–
Worcestershire	28	18	3	6	1	0	5	191
Warwickshire	28	14	5	9	0	0	5	150
Northamptonshire	28	12	4	11	1	0	5	130
Surrey	28	11	3	13	1	0	9	129
Yorkshire	28	11	3	14	0	0	8	126
Middlesex	28	9	6	12	1	2	9	112
Kent	28	9	6	12	1	3	6	108
Somerset	28	8	8	8	4	4	4	96
Sussex	28	8	9	10	1	1	3	88
Essex	28	7	11	8	2	5	3	86
Glamorgan	28	7	7	12	2	1	6	84
Derbyshire	28	5	9	12	2	4	5	68
Hampshire	28	5	8	14	1	1	5	68
Lancashire	28	4	10	13	1	4	8	64
Nottinghamshire	28	4	13	11	0	3	4	54
Leicestershire	28	3	18	5	2	7	0	44
Gloucestershire	28	3	15	10	0	2	4	43

Surrey and Worcestershire records include one point for tie on first innings in match drawn.
Gloucestershire and Hampshire records include one point for tie on first innings in match lost.
Hampshire gained five points in drawn match when scores finished level and they were batting.

1965
County Championship

BATTING AVERAGES

Batsman	No. of Innings	Times Not Out	Highest Score	Total Runs	Average
G. Boycott	28	1	95	942	34·88
J.H. Hampshire	43	3	110*	1102	27·55
R. Illingworth	41	8	90	810	24·54
D.B. Close	41	6	101*	850	24·28
P.J. Sharpe	46	4	100	991	23·59
K. Taylor	34	2	86	714	22·31
D.E.V. Padgett	47	0	81	972	20·68
J.G. Binks	37	7	59	584	19·46
R.A. Hutton	29	5	91	464	19·33
F.S. Trueman	32	1	101	541	17·45
J.C. Balderstone	14	1	51	213	16·38
A.G. Nicholson	21	15	12	60	10·00
D. Wilson	34	8	37	228	8·76

The following also batted:
J.P.G. Chadwick 59, 4, 8*, 1 and 0*;
J.S. Waring 0*, 0, 6*, 6*, 0*, 3* and 3;
D.L. Ash 12, 0 and 10;
M. Ryan 11 and 0.

*Signifies not out.

1965
County Championship

BOWLING AVERAGES

Bowler	Overs	Maidens	Runs	Wickets	Average
F.S. Trueman	568	140	1307	115	11·36
R. Illingworth	663·3	292	1150	71	16·19
M. Ryan	37	10	88	5	17·60
D. Wilson	578	243	1133	64	17·70
R.A. Hutton	424·4	101	1083	58	18·67
A.G. Nicholson	446·3	154	890	47	18·93
J.C. Balderstone	94	43	172	9	19·11
D.B. Close	445·2	177	1052	48	21·91
J.S. Waring	128	33	348	15	23·20
The following also bowled:					
G. Boycott	31	16	38	2	
K. Taylor	32	10	76	2	
D.E.V. Padgett	6	4	6	1	
J.H. Hampshire	12	0	56	0	
D.L. Ash	11	7	22	0	
P.J. Sharpe	4	1	17	0	
J.P.G. Chadwick	2	0	9	0	
J.G. Binks	2	0	12	0	

1965
County Championship

FINAL POSITIONS

	P	W	L	D	No dec.	1st inns. lead in match L	1st inns. lead in match D	Pts.
Points awarded	–	12	–	–	–	2	2	–
Worcestershire	28	13	4	10	1	1	6	144
Northamptonshire	28	13	4	9	2	0	5	140
Glamorgan	28	12	6	8	2	2	4	132
Yorkshire	28	9	4	14	1	1	11	114
Kent	28	8	5	14	1	0	8	96
Middlesex	28	8	7	12	1	0	7	94
Somerset	28	8	11	8	1	2	4	92
Surrey	28	7	4	15	2	1	8	92
Derbyshire	28	7	9	11	1	2	6	86
Gloucestershire	28	7	8	11	2	1	5	82
Warwickshire	28	5	5	18	0	1	9	70
Hampshire	28	5	4	17	2	0	8	66
Lancashire	28	5	13	9	1	0	5	60
Leicestershire	28	5	11	11	1	2	2	58
Essex	28	4	7	16	1	0	7	54
Sussex	28	4	10	14	0	2	4	52
Nottinghamshire	28	3	11	13	1	3	6	48

Surrey's record includes six points for first innings lead in match restricted by rain to last third of time allotted.

1966
County Championship

BATTING AVERAGES

Batsman	No. of Innings	Times Not Out	Highest Score	Total Runs	Average
G. Boycott	31	3	164	1097	39·17
D.B. Close	43	8	115*	1056	30·17
D.E.V. Padgett	45	4	79	1054	25·70
J.H. Hampshire	44	4	78	992	24·80
R. Illingworth	31	7	98*	572	23·83
K. Taylor	41	2	87	881	22·58
P.J. Sharpe	43	3	72	870	21·75
J. Waring	10	6	26	78	19·50
D. Wilson	39	6	52	527	15·96
J.C. Balderstone	13	1	64	183	15·25
J.G. Binks	37	8	42	383	13·26
F.S. Trueman	37	3	43	409	12·02
A.G. Nicholson	25	15	41	120	12·00
R.A. Hutton	6	1	16	40	8·00

The following also batted:
B. Leadbeater 1, 2, 4 and 7;
G.A. Cope 2, 0, 1*, 1 and 3*;
C. Old 3 and 0.

*Signifies not out.

1966
County Championship

BOWLING AVERAGES

Bowler	Overs	Maidens	Runs	Wickets	Average
R. Illingworth	631·4	240	1234	85	14·51
A.G. Nicholson	822·3	282	1581	105	15·05
D. Wilson	723	289	1443	87	16·58
F.S. Trueman	755·3	182	1732	101	17·14
D.B. Close	441·3	172	979	40	20·39
R.A. Hutton	63	15	176	8	20·00
J. Waring	145·5	36	367	16	22·93
The following also bowled:					
J.C. Balderstone	28·1	6	84	3	
G.A. Cope	36	16	58	0	
J.H. Hampshire	22	4	76	0	
K. Taylor	6	2	13	0	
G. Boycott	5	2	4	0	
C. Old	2	1	8	0	

1966
County Championship

FINAL POSITIONS

	P	W	L	D	No dec.	1st inns. lead	Pts.
Points awarded	–	10	–	–	–	2	–
Yorkshire	28	15	5	8	0	17	184
Worcestershire	28	13	5	9	1	18	166
Somerset	28	13	7	7	1	13	156
Kent	28	11	8	8	1	17	144
Northamptonshire	28	10	9	9	0	15	130
Warwickshire	28	8	8	10	2	16	113
Surrey	28	8	3	16	1	15	110
Leicestershire	28	8	7	12	1	14	108
Derbyshire	28	8	12	7	1	8	96
Sussex	28	6	11	11	0	16	92
Hampshire	28	5	4	18	1	16	87
Lancashire	28	6	11	8	3	13	86
Middlesex	28	6	5	14	3	13	86
Glamorgan	28	6	8	13	1	10	85
Gloucestershire	28	6	12	9	1	7	75
Essex	28	4	10	11	3	10	60
Nottinghamshire	28	3	11	12	2	8	46

Warwickshire and Gloucestershire records include one point each for tie in first innings.
Hampshire and Glamorgan records include five points in drawn match when scores finished level and they were batting.

1967
County Championship

BATTING AVERAGES

Batsman	No. of Innings	Times Not Out	Highest Score	Total Runs	Average
G. Boycott	28	2	220*	1260	48·46
D.B. Close	19	2	98	585	34·41
D.E.V. Padgett	40	5	139	1103	31·51
R. Illingworth	24	6	65*	537	29·83
P.J. Sharpe	39	5	93	1012	29·76
J.H. Hampshire	39	5	102	922	27·11
K. Taylor	37	2	162	723	20·65
J.G. Binks	28	3	70*	497	19·88
J.C. Balderstone	11	1	71	193	19·30
D. Wilson	32	6	52	478	18·38
C. Old	8	1	45	124	17·71
P. Stringer	5	4	8*	14	14·00
F.S. Trueman	28	3	34	307	12·28
R.A. Hutton	11	2	33	105	11·66
A.G. Nicholson	20	6	33	100	7·14
B. Leadbeater	5	1	14	26	6·50
G.A. Cope	10	4	15*	25	4·16

*Signifies not out.

1967
County Championship

BOWLING AVERAGES

Bowler	Overs	Maidens	Runs	Wickets	Average
G.A. Cope	218·3	106	409	32	12·78
A.G. Nicholson	663·3	187	1511	90	16·78
R. Illingworth	555·1	219	1075	63	17·06
C. Old	119·3	28	352	20	17·60
D. Wilson	612·4	260	1128	63	17·90
F.S. Trueman	476·1	107	1296	57	22·73
R.A. Hutton	162	40	468	16	29·25
P. Stringer	94	31	236	8	29·50
D.B. Close	203·1	68	508	13	39·07
The following also bowled:					
J.C. Balderstone	25	9	50	5	
K. Taylor	56	15	132	2	
D.E.V. Padgett	8	6	6	1	
P.J. Sharpe	6	2	14	1	
G. Boycott	10	1	35	1	
J.H. Hampshire	44	10	139		
J.G. Binks	2		8		

1967
County Championship

FINAL POSITIONS

	P	W	L	D	Tie	No. dec.	1st Inn. lead	Pts.
Points awarded	–	8	–	2	4	–	4	–
Yorkshire	28	12	5	9	0	2	18	186
Kent	28	11	3	12	0	2	16	176
Leicestershire	28	10	3	12	0	3	18	176
Surrey	28	8	4	12	0	4	15	148
Worcestershire	28	6	6	16	0	0	13	132
Derbyshire	28	5	5	17	0	1	14	130
Middlesex	28	5	4	14	1	4	14	128
Somerset	28	5	7	14	0	2	13	120
Northamptonshire	28	7	8	11	0	2	10	118
Warwickshire	28	5	4	15	0	4	11	118
Lancashire	28	4	3	17	0	4	12	116
Hampshire	28	5	6	13	1	3	10	114
Sussex	28	5	9	12	0	2	10	104
Glamorgan	28	4	7	15	0	2	9	100
Essex	28	3	9	14	0	2	9	88
Nottinghamshire	28	0	4	22	0	2	11	88
Gloucestershire	28	3	11	9	0	5	11	86

The Warwickshire and Hampshire records include four points instead of two in drawn matches when scores finished level and they were batting.

The Lancashire, Glamorgan, Warwickshire and Hampshire records include two points for a tie in the first innings.

1968
County Championship

BATTING AVERAGES

Batsman	No. of Innings	Times Not Out	Highest Score	Total Runs	Average
G. Boycott	15	5	180*	774	77·40
P.J. Sharpe	42	8	143*	1102	32·41
R. Illingworth	26	7	100*	586	30·84
J.H. Hampshire	39	5	100	952	28·00
D.E.V. Padgett	39	2	136*	984	26·59
D.B. Close	28	6	77*	536	24·36
K. Taylor	37	3	85	712	20·94
A.G. Nicholson	19	12	43	98	14·00
D. Wilson	35	8	61*	372	13·77
G.A. Cope	6	2	17*	54	13·50
B. Leadbeater	6	2	13*	52	13·00
J.G. Binks	31	2	52*	374	12·89
F.S. Trueman	25	4	45	263	12·52
J.C. Balderstone	9	–	45	111	12·33
R.A. Hutton	23	4	31*	187	9·84
C.M. Old	6	1	14	29	5·80

The following also batted:
P. Stringer 2, 8*, 15*;
J. Woodford 34, 2, 1.   *Signifies not out.

1968
County Championship

BOWLING AVERAGES

Bowler	Overs	Maidens	Runs	Wickets	Average
G.A. Cope	92·5	30	211	20	10·55
D. Wilson	719·4	299	1275	102	12·50
R. Illingworth	585·5	208	1178	86	13·69
A.G. Nicholson	614	211	1269	80	15·86
D.B Close	251	118	500	24	20·83
R.A. Hutton	365	76	1027	49	20·95
F.S. Trueman	404·1	93	1017	46	22·10
C.M. Old	96·4	20	216	6	36·00
The following also bowled:					
P. Stringer	41	12	117	5	
J.H. Hampshire	10	1	26	1	
K. Taylor	51	15	125	3	
G. Boycott	2	0	10		
P.J. Sharpe	1		1	1	
D.E.V. Padgett	1		11		
J.C. Balderstone	24	10	58	2	

1968
County Championship

FINAL POSITIONS

	P	W	L	D	A	Bt.	Bwl.	Pts.
						Bonus points		
Points awarded	–	10	–	–	–	–	–	–
Yorkshire	28	11	4	13	0	46	114	270
Kent	28	12	5	11	0	41	95	256
Glamorgan	28	11	6	9	2	42	85	237
Nottinghamshire	28	7	3	17	1	53	99	222
Hampshire	28	8	5	15	0	43	92	215
Lancashire	28	8	6	14	0	24	105	209
Worcestershire	28	8	7	13	0	26	97	203
Derbyshire	28	6	5	16	1	47	92	199
Leicestershire	28	6	10	12	0	52	85	197
Middlesex	28	8	6	14	0	21	91	192
Warwickshire	28	7	8	12	1	38	82	190
Somerset	28	5	11	11	1	36	86	172
Northamptonshire	28	5	6	17	0	34	86	170
Essex	28	5	6	16	1	31	88	169
Surrey	28	4	7	17	0	25	92	157
Gloucestershire	28	2	8	17	1	40	93	153
Sussex	28	2	12	14	0	43	77	140

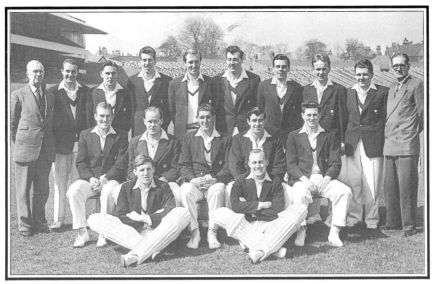

1960 L-R, back row: C. Turner (scorer), Bolus, Padgett, D. Wilson, Platt, Ryan, Bird, Birkenshaw, Sharpe, G. Allcock (masseur). Seated: Illingworth, Close, V. Wilson, Trueman, Binks. Front: Taylor, Stott. (Photo by Telegraph & Argus, Bradford)

1968 L-R, Boycott, Binks, Padgett, Illingworth, Trueman, Close, Wilson, Sharpe, Nicholson, Taylor, Hampshire. (Photo by Telegraph & Argus, Bradford)

1963. L-R, back row: Hampshire, Wilson, John Waring, Ryan, Taylor, Padgett, Sharpe. Front: Binks, Trueman, Close, Illingworth, Stott. (Photo by S. Hunt)

Gillette Cup finalists 1969. L-R, back row: Balderstone, Hampshire, Nicholson, Hutton, Old, Boycott, Cope. Front: Sharpe, Binks, Close, Padgett, Wilson. (Photo by Telegraph & Argus, Bradford)

1967 L-R, back row: Cope, Sharpe, Nicholson, Stringer, Waring, Hampshire, Boycott. Front: Padgett, Binks, Trueman, Close, Illingworth, Taylor, Wilson. (Photo by Telegraph & Argus, Bradford)

Yorkshire cricketers show off their new Terylene raincoats in the 1960 season. (Photo by Telegraph & Argus, Bradford)

Fred Trueman prepares for the Aussies in 1963. (Photo by Telephoto)

Acknowledgements

Photographs for chapter head pages taken by:

Telegraph and Argus (4, 6, 7, 18, 19, 21, 22)
Yorkshire Post (8, 9, 12. 14, 15)
G.P. Herringshaw (5, 13, 17)
Photo Press, Leeds (3, 10, 11, 16)
S&G Press Agency (2)
S. Hunt (20)
Unknown (1)